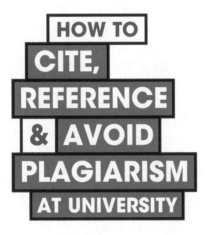

HOW TO
CITE,
REFERENCE
& AVOID
PLAGIARISM
AT UNIVERSITY

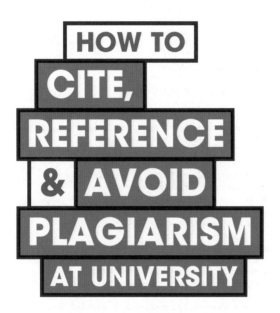

HOW TO CITE, REFERENCE & AVOID PLAGIARISM AT UNIVERSITY

**KATHLEEN McMILLAN &
JONATHAN WEYERS**

Harlow, England • London • New York • Boston • San Francisco • Toronto • Sydney
Auckland • Singapore • Hong Kong • Tokyo • Seoul • Taipei • New Delhi
Cape Town • São Paulo • Mexico City • Madrid • Amsterdam • Munich • Paris • Milan

Pearson Education Limited
Edinburgh Gate
Harlow
Essex CM20 2JE
England

and Associated Companies throughout the world

Visit us on the World Wide Web at:
www.perason.com/uk

First published 2013 (print and electronic)

ISBN: 978-0-273-77333-7 (print)
ISBN: 978-0-273-77336-8 (epub)

British Library Cataloguing-in-Publication Data
A catalogue record for this book is available from the British Library

Library of Congress Cataloging-in-Publication Data
A catalog record for this book is available from the Library of Congress

10 9 8 7 6 5 4 3 2 1
16 15 14 13 12

Typeset in 9.5/13pt Helvetica Neue Pro Roman by 3
Printed and bound in Great Britain by Henry Ling Ltd, Dorchester, Dorset

SMARTER STUDY SKILLS

Instant answers to your most pressing university skills problems and queries

Are there any secrets to successful study?

The simple answer is 'yes' – there are some essential skills, tips and techniques that can help you to improve your performance and success in all areas of your university studies.

These handy, easy-to-use guides to the most common areas where most students need help, provide accessible, straightforward practical tips and instant solutions that provide you with the tools and techniques that will enable you to improve your performance and get better results – and better grades!

Each book in the series allows you to assess and address a particular set of skills and strategies, in crucial areas of your studies. Each book then delivers practical, no-nonsense tips, techniques and strategies that will enable you to significantly improve your abilities and performance in time to make a difference.

The books in the series are:

- *How to Write Essays & Assignments*
- *How to Write Dissertations & Project Reports*
- *How to Argue*
- *How to Improve your Maths Skills*
- *How to Use Statistics*
- *How to Succeed in Exams & Assessments*
- *How to Cite, Reference & Avoid Plagiarism at University*
- *How to Improve Your Critical Thinking & Reflective Skills*

For a complete handbook covering all of these study skills and more:

- *The Study Skills Book*

Get smart, get a head start!

CONTENTS

FIVE REFERENCING STYLES

APPENDICES

PREFACE AND ACKNOWLEDGEMENTS

We're pleased that you've chosen *How to Cite, Reference and Avoid Plagiarism at University* and we hope that it will help you to cite and reference with confidence in your academic work. The aim is to give you the understanding, language and thinking tools so that you can use the work of others appropriately and with correct attribution. Once learnt, correct citation becomes part of an academic writer's toolset and is part of the intellectual development that marks your ability to think critically. We have broken the process down into different elements that explain how to manage your sources and your writing so that you produce work that has academic integrity and ensure that no inadvertent plagiarism appears. We hope that it will meet your needs – regardless of your experience and background.

We would like to offer our sincere thanks to many people who have influenced us and contributed to the development and production of this book. Numerous students over the years have helped us to test our ideas, especially those whose written work we have commented upon, supervised and assessed. We are grateful to the following colleagues and friends who have helped us directly or indirectly: Margaret Adamson, Michael Allardice, the late John Berridge, Stuart Cross, Margaret Forest, Andy Jackson, Bill Kirton, Eric Monaghan, Neil Paterson, Jane Prior, Fiona O'Donnell, Dorothy Smith, Gordon Spark, Amanda Whitehead, David Walker and David Wishart. Also, we acknowledge those at other universities who have helped frame our thoughts, particularly our good friends Rob Reed, Nicki Hedge and Esther Daborn. We owe a special debt to the senior colleagues who encouraged various projects that contributed to this book, and who allowed us the freedom to pursue this avenue of scholarship, especially Robin Adamson, Chris Carter, Ian Francis, Rod Herbert and David Swinfen. At Pearson Education, we have had excellent advice and support from Steve Temblett, Rob Cottee and Joy Cash. Finally, we would like to say thanks to our long-suffering but nevertheless enthusiastic families, Derek, Keith, Nolwenn, Fiona, Tom and Eilidh; and Mary, Paul and James, all of whom helped in various capacities.

We hope that you will find this a useful resource and that it will support your learning and development as an academic writer. We would be delighted to hear your opinion of the book, any suggestions you have for additions and improvements, and especially if you feel that it has made a positive difference to your confidence in writing, whatever your academic purpose.

Kathleen McMillan and Jonathan Weyers

HOW TO USE THIS BOOK

Each chapter in *How to Cite, Reference and Avoid Plagiarism at University* has been organised and designed to be as clear and simple as possible. The chapters are self-contained and deal with particular aspects of the subject matter so that you can read the book through from beginning to end, or in sections, or dip into specific chapters as you need them.

At the start of each chapter you'll find a brief paragraph and a **Key topics** list that let you know what is included. There is also a list of **Key terms** at this point that highlights words that may be new to you or may be used in a particular way in the chapter. Should you be uncertain about the meaning of these words, you will find definitions in the **Glossary** at the end of the book.

Within each chapter, the text is laid out to help you absorb the key concepts easily, using headings and bulleted lists to enable you to find what you need. Relevant examples are contained in figures, tables and boxes which complement the text. The inset boxes are of three types:

Smart tip boxes emphasise key advice that we think will be particularly useful to you.

Information boxes provide additional information that will broaden your understanding by giving examples and definitions.

Query boxes raise questions for you to consider about your personal approach to the topic.

At the end of each chapter, there's a **Practical tips** section with additional suggestions for action. You should regard this as a menu from which to select the ideas that appeal to you and your learning style.

Finally, the **And now** section provides three suggestions for possible follow-up action as you consider ideas further.

INTRODUCTION

1

THE IMPORTANCE OF CORRECT CITATION AND REFERENCING

How to understand the conventions of academic writing

Writing for academic purposes is challenging and fulfilling. It brings together your knowledge and understanding of a topic – but it is more than that. From your writing, you will gain an ability to use language effectively in communicating your ideas, as well as an ability to communicate the ideas of others as you use these to frame your own discussion. Thus, being able to understand what it means to cite sources and how to do this properly is essential to your success as an academic author.

KEY TOPICS

→ What is plagiarism?

→ What is citation?

→ What is referencing?

→ What are the advantages of avoiding plagiarism?

→ An overview of the processes required for successful citation and referencing

KEY TERMS

Attribute Bibliography Citation Intellectual property Paraphrasing Plagiarism Quotation Reference list Referencing Summarising

The development of electronic global communication networks has raised significant issues within the academic world. More than at any time in academic history, comprehensive and growing databases allow access to a far wider range of multi-level source material that students can use to support their own writing. Specifically, the potential for immediate electronic access to academic publications has produced benefits in terms of widening knowledge and understanding in specialist fields and has brought resources and publications more readily within the public domain. In addition, wide-ranging interpersonal communications have contributed to debate in many fields and using many media. Therefore, students and researchers have, at their fingertips, an array of material which can be used to support their own learning and writing. Clearly, this has many accessibility and time-saving advantages, but also brings the risk of plagiarism closer.

WHAT IS PLAGIARISM?

Academic authors demonstrate their scholarship by writing and publishing in their own fields. They have the moral right to claim such work as their own property (sometimes referred to as 'intellectual property'). Hence, the academic community requires that academic authors, whether undergraduate, postgraduate or researcher, attribute the ownership of ideas, text and other forms of work to the original writers. The word and its verb form are defined in the Information box opposite.

WHAT IS CITATION?

In the academic environment at university level, citation involves linking an idea within a new text to information or data derived from another source document and its author(s). This gives recognition to the original author by providing sufficient information from the publication details so that the reader can locate the original document, if they wish. Integration of the ideas of others can be done:

- by direct quotation, that is, writing down what they wrote word for word; or
- by paraphrasing the idea in words that are different from those of the original author.

Whichever of these methods is adopted, the actual attribution in the text, namely, the publishing details, will follow the citation and referencing style required for your writing. Styles of citation and referencing are explained and outlined in **Chs 10–15**. The word and its verb form are defined in the Information box opposite.

Defining terms

To clarify our use of some terms and to avoid any confusion, the following are provided as dictionary definitions of expressions as used in this book:

Citation (noun) • a quotation (a book, its author, or a passage from it) as an example or a proof • mentioning as an example or illustration.

To cite (verb) • to use a phrase or sentence from a piece of writing or speech, especially in order to support or prove something.

Reference (noun) • a direction in a book to another passage or another book where information can be found • a book or passage referred to • the act of referring to a book or passage for information.

To reference (verb) • to mention a particular writer or piece of work • to create a list of all the books that are mentioned in a piece of academic writing.

Plagiarism (noun) • the process of taking another person's work, ideas, or words and using them as if they were your own.

To plagiarise (verb) • to take someone else's work, ideas, or words and use them as if they were your own.

(Note: British English spelling)   (Source: *www.macmillandictionary.com*)

WHAT IS REFERENCING?

There are two usages in the context of academic writing:

1 providing information in the text about authorship of the original source material; and

2 providing the publication details in some kind of footnote, reference list or bibliography in accordance with the citation and referencing style being followed (**Chs 11–15**).

The rationale for this is:

● to protect the 'intellectual property' of the original author; and

● to provide readers with specific bibliographical information.

The word and its verb form are defined in the Information box above.

To place this in context, Figures 1.1 and 1.2 show a layout for a scientific journal paper and for a social sciences academic paper

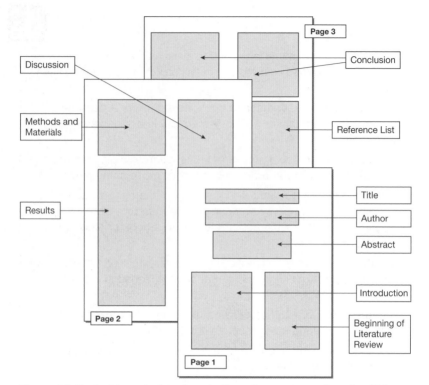

Figure 1.1 Typical layout of a paper in the sciences or engineering. This paper might appear in an academic journal where the text is usually printed in columns. The pages read from front to back and show a standard presentation: *Title, Author, Abstract, Introduction, Literature Review, Methods and Materials, Results, Discussion and Conclusion, followed by References.* Pages are simply to illustrate layout; more pages would be the norm for a journal article. Length is usually given by word count.

respectively so that you can see how all of this applies in practice. Further, explicit printed examples are provided throughout the book.

WHY IS AVOIDING PLAGIARISM IMPORTANT?

There are two intertwined strands to avoiding plagiarism:

1 the need to maintain your academic integrity, that is, your honesty, by giving correct attribution to sources; and
2 the need to demonstrate your critical thinking skills, namely, your ability to analyse complex information.

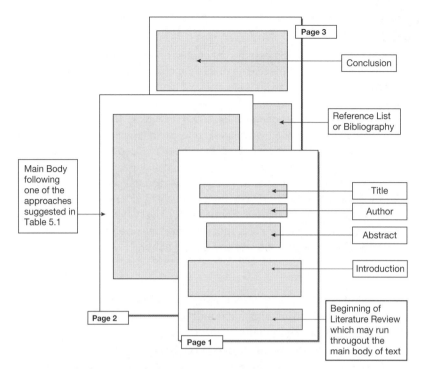

Figure 1.2 **Sample layout of a paper in the Social Sciences.** These papers are less strictly divided than in the natural sciences, for example. A suggested order might be: *Title, Author, Abstract (if appropriate), Introduction, Main Body, Conclusion, Reference List (or Bibliography)*. Pages are simply to illustrate layout; more pages would be the norm for a journal article. Length is usually given by word count.

Therefore, by learning to structure and present your views with appropriate attention to the published evidence, you enhance the quality of your research and acknowledge the contribution of others to the literature. Thus, learning how to cite and reference is essential to successful academic writing and will help you to achieve the highest of assessed standards in your work.

AN OVERVIEW OF THE PROCESSES REQUIRED FOR SUCCESSFUL CITATION AND REFERENCING

Many citation and referencing systems exist and, over time, some have been modified to create an even wider array of similar and, at times,

i Critical thinking

Some students do not grasp the concept of critical thinking – in general terms, it is the ability to evaluate opinion and evidence systematically, clearly and with purpose. In the context of citation, it is part of the process where students examine a range of the existing literature which they then evaluate for accuracy, logic and relevance. This provides the evidence for the writer's own analysis or exploration of a topic or issue. Thus, the notion that, to be critical, thinking expressed in academic text must be entirely the author's own work is a mistaken one, but it is one of the reasons that students do not acknowledge the source of text or ideas. People often interpret the words 'critical' and 'criticism' to mean being negative about an issue. For university level work, the alternative meaning of 'making a careful judgement after balanced consideration of all aspects of a topic' is the one you should adopt.

competing systems. Sometimes students are instructed to follow one of these particular styles of citation and referencing, for example, Harvard or Vancouver; sometimes students are left to choose a style for themselves. At this point, students become almost entirely focused on layout and punctuation of the nominated style – the 'mechanics' of the style – without really understanding that there is more to following the academic conventions than slavish devotion to pressing the punctuation keys in the right places or indiscriminate sprinkling of their writing with citations. Indeed, where there is a suggestion that a student might have presented work that is plagiarised, often there is confusion and not a small degree of indignation because all the full-stops and commas have been correctly positioned or the requisite number of citations has been inserted – so where is the plagiarism?

In response to this question, this book aims to tackle these and similar misunderstandings. The book is divided into five distinct parts that explore the nature of citation and referencing, in relationship to plagiarism and in application. The intention is to lead the reader on a journey towards understanding the underpinning principles of citation in a logical, step by step approach. This will mean that you acquire full control of the skills of quotation, summarising and paraphrasing so that plagiarism just does not become a consideration.

In this, the **Introduction** section, the outline of the book is explained. In **Key concepts of citation, referencing and plagiarism**, the journey begins with closer examination of plagiarism. We consider some of the facts (**Ch 2**) and then debunk some prevalent myths and misunderstandings by showing plagiarism in its many guises (**Ch 3**).

Having addressed and put aside the issues surrounding plagiarism, we move on to practical aspects of learning how to achieve sound citation and referencing in your work. This begins with basic steps in researching and evaluating sources from the literature, appraising the content, constructing the framework of your understanding and assessing how technology can assist in handling references (**Ch 4**).

At the next stage in drafting text, a writer has to achieve an understanding of the principles and practical aspects of using the work of others to evidence their own writing. In **Chapter 5** we analyse the composition of academic texts to identify how writers construct discussion within a text and how this impacts on their choices regarding material to be included in their own work. We then provide examples of particular language strategies to present the ideas of others as part of a discussion on the topic (**Ch 6**).

As noted, citation can be provided by direct quotation and the particular aspects of how to do this in academic writing can be found in **Chapter 7**. The alternative approach to citation entailing expression of the relevant material from sources in words that are not those of the original authors, requires strategies for summarising and paraphrasing; these are explained and modelled in **Chapter 8**.

Learning these sophisticated skills should not be done in the abstract, since these are best assimilated by experience underpinned by a clear understanding of how to apply the three strategies in context. Therefore, in the third section, **A case study of citing and referencing**, an example is used to draw together the processes, strategies and their application as explained in earlier chapters (**Ch 9**). This takes a single theme and shows the entire process from selection of source material to final text. This practical example replicates the steps in critical thinking that writers need to follow in order to draw on cited evidence to support their position by making use of quotation, summary and paraphrase to attribute the work of others correctly.

To describe the full diversity of styles in existence would be impractical as there are many variants. Therefore, in the fourth section, **Conventions and terminology of citations and references**, we provide information about how styles can be categorised, their terminology and the particular 'quirks' of presentation, language and grammar that distinguish some styles (**Ch 10**). Detailed examples for five of the styles more commonly followed in university environments are then provided in **Chapters 11, 12, 13, 14** and **15**. In each illustration, you will find a sample text that models the use of the specific citing and referencing system, and any corresponding footnoting, reference listing or bibliography as appropriate. Finally, any particular characteristics relating to grammar, presentation or layout are also presented. The **Appendix** includes guidelines on punctuation for citing and referencing, and a review of common grammar points. Spelling rules are also revisited.

Where we have used authentic text to provide examples, we have cited these accordingly. However, sometimes we have found that creating tailored texts allowed us to illustrate points more effectively with content that did not distract by its complexity. Thus, some 'citations' used in these texts are pure invention and so do not appear in the list of references for this book. For continuity, within the text of this book in sections 1 to 4, we follow the Harvard style since it is one of the simpler and more commonly used styles.

PRACTICAL TIPS FOR DEVELOPING AWARENESS OF STYLE CONVENTIONS IN CITING AND REFERENCING

Follow a standard style. Styles of citation and referencing can vary from institution to institution, from department to department and sometimes even within the same department as well as from discipline to discipline. When a style is recommended to you by name, then it is important to follow this style. However, first, you need to ascertain how that style has been interpreted in your department or institution since, for various reasons, some styles have deviated from their 'official' formats, for example, with minor punctuation alterations. You should always follow the interpretation given in your handbook or guidelines.

Select a style. If you decide to adopt a style of your own choice, first of all, always check your course handbook or guidance to authors provided by many publishing houses or journal editorial boards, since these usually provide very specific guidance on their preferred citation and referencing style. Where no style is recommended, then go to a reputable journal in your subject area and identify the style adopted there. This should give you some indication of what style would be acceptable in your own area.

GO AND NOW . . .

1.1 Look again at Figures 1.1 and 1.2. By the time that you have read this chapter, you should have a better appreciation of the way that academic writing differs from writing in a novel or a newspaper. Academic writing should be based on sound evidence and objective analysis using a more formal style of language. Look at Figures 1.1 and 1.2 with this in mind so that you become more aware of the style of writing that you may have to read – and probably, in the longer term, produce.

1.2 Visit the Appendix section at the end of this book. A read-through of the content will show you the extent of supportive information that is provided to help you read and use this book efficiently and which you can consult for application in your own writing.

1.3 Consult the Glossary for definitions for this chapter. In that section (pages 178–82), you will find the words that are listed as the key terms in each chapter. It is worth checking each term to confirm that your understanding of the term coincides with its use in the context of plagiarism, citation and referencing.

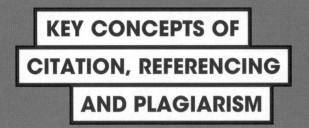

KEY CONCEPTS OF CITATION, REFERENCING AND PLAGIARISM

2

FACTS ABOUT PLAGIARISM

How this form of academic dishonesty occurs and how it can be identified

The subject of plagiarism is often discussed in judgemental and negative terms – for example, using words such as 'cheating', 'detection', 'punishment' and 'unethical'. The purpose of this book is not to accuse writers of dishonesty, but to offer solutions to a potential problem. This chapter considers some of the facts that surround 'plagiarism' and its strong overtones of dishonesty so that you can understand the negative perspectives it engenders in the academic community.

KEY TOPICS

➔ Respecting academic conventions on intellectual property

➔ Implications of plagiarism

➔ Reasons for plagiarism

➔ How plagiarism can be identified

➔ How academics can counter plagiarism

KEY TERMS

Copyright   Intellectual property   Objectivity   Paper mill   Peer-review
Subjectivity   Syntax   Unethical

Academic literature is produced after extensive study of existing publications and developed through applied or theoretical research into a topic. That process entitles academics to claim that work as their intellectual property – much the same way as identifying a car as an item of property. In the same way that car owners would not expect their cars to be stolen, so too academic authors do not expect their work to be stolen.

RESPECTING ACADEMIC CONVENTIONS ON INTELLECTUAL PROPERTY

The convention has developed that academics in their own writing cite the work of others to respect the original thinking and consequent ownership of that work – colloquially, sometimes referred to using the legal term, intellectual property (IP). Therefore, the convention shows respect being paid to those individuals whose research, writings and other work created the source cited. Hence, whether they are undergraduates, postgraduates or researchers, all academic authors are expected to follow this convention. To fail to do so is considered unethical.

IMPLICATIONS OF PLAGIARISM

Institutions and the departments or schools within them have come to recognise the need to mark out their ethical position by having a formal code of practice on plagiarism while some require students to sign a disclaimer on their work to the effect that the work is entirely of their own making.

Nevertheless, plagiarism occurs – not only among the undergraduate population but also within the academic world and beyond. Some notable cases have been reported where the use of search engines, for example, has exposed instances of plagiarism years after the plagiarism occurred. Whatever the circumstances, the negative consequences can be seriously damaging – shame, loss of professional status, loss of job, loss of marks, loss of degree and even expulsion from the institution. Thus, the pressure on academic authors not to plagiarise is significant and yet some people take the risk of jeopardising their future careers by plagiarising the work of others.

REASONS FOR PLAGIARISM

Plagiarism is a global problem and one which can arise because of different social, economic and academic pressures. These remain a matter of surmise but may include:

- **Unfamiliarity with academic texts** – not knowing what an academic paper should look like since textbooks used at school or college level generally do not use citation, therefore, university may be new students' first exposure to the genres of academic writing.

- **Stress** – pressure of work and shortage of time that arise from having to do paid work to pay tuition fees and cost of living.

- **Fear of failure** – perceptions of the need to do well in the eyes of family and peers, in the case of students, and the emphasis on the requirement to maintain a steady flow of publication, in the case of the professional academic.

- **Speed** – internet sources mean that text can be copied quickly and so the 'writing' can be produced quickly and efficiently, but without any deep understanding or learning taking place, meaning that it seems easier and generally more expedient to 'cut and paste'.

- **Cultural differences** – if students have come from a learning environment where 'copying from the book' is rewarded or where using the work of learned authorities is a form of flattery, the concept of academic integrity is sometimes difficult to absorb.

- **Weak research skills** – some people enter higher education with little experience of seeking material for themselves and are unsure of how to go about developing the skill of research as part of the expected self-directed study strategies.

- **Ease of access to cyber-providers** – sometimes called 'paper mills', these providers claim to provide complete essays, dissertations, and even doctoral theses, to order. A lucrative growth industry has emerged on the internet because some people are willing to pay for others to do their work. The costs are considerable and there is no guarantee of quality or indication that the purchased work has not been plagiarised at the time of its creation. Clearly, these works could be sold many times over thus increasing the risk of identified plagiarism for those who buy these products.

- **Ease of access to plagiarism detection software on the wider Web** – sites exist where sophisticated software can be used (at a price) to enable student writers to submit their papers electronically to identify plagiarism. The feedback provides information about extent of plagiarism, and identifies specific sections of plagiarised text. In some cases, recommendations of how to rectify these sections are given.

- **Difficulty in expressing ideas in writing** – some writers find it difficult to express complex ideas in their own words or they do not feel confident in use of techniques to construct a discussion on paper; some feel that their efforts would be too poor to submit and contend that they could not improve on the writing of an established authority.

- **Apparent dishonesty** – some people simply regard plagiarism as acceptable. Furthermore, plagiarists often go to excessive lengths in time and effort to avoid having to produce assignments for themselves; were they to concentrate on doing the work honestly in the first place, then the risk of plagiarism could be avoided. That said, there are instances where what seems like dishonesty, for example, deliberate copying from the source without acknowledgement, is an attempt to camouflage perceived literacy and intellectual shortcomings.

HOW PLAGIARISM CAN BE IDENTIFIED

Experienced academics and editors can often instinctively detect plagiarised text quite easily. For example, any text produced for academic purposes without any attributions at all (**Ch 9**) will be less likely to be accepted as a serious piece of work and could imply either that the author has provided a subjective uncorroborated piece of text, or that the text has come from a printed source such as a textbook (or several textbooks). By contrast, texts that are littered with references in a haphazard fashion are just as likely to be criticised for lack of rigour and draw attention to probable plagiarism.

Other signs of plagiarism may show:

- a style of writing and language that is not consistent throughout the document; the 'linguistic fingerprints' of a text may identify that the work of more than one source has been used. In other words, the 'joins show';
- language that is too perfect; the style of writing may not align with the level at which the writer is studying;
- hypertext links that have been left in the copied and pasted text;
- an introduction and a conclusion that do not correspond;
- repetition of errors in the plagiarised form where these were present in the original text;
- use of different citation styles over the text;
- differences in font style and point sizes of the text; or

- text drawn directly from the work of the academic to whom the text is submitted or from the work of a third party known to them both – could be a colleague or a peer.

HOW ACADEMICS COUNTER PLAGIARISM

Where any of the above 'clues' suggest plagiarism, a simple Google-type search can often throw up a close match to the exact text used to prompt the search, as well as to further matched text employed by the plagiarist. However, many universities have bought into 'text managing software' in attempts to counter acts of plagiarism. Consequently, institutions and academics can arrange for submitted text to be run automatically through this kind of program. The companies who market such software stress that it does not locate plagiarism. Instead, as they point out, it simply matches the incidence of strings of the same or similar words used in more than one text after checking a wide database of sources. Nevertheless, a high 'matching' score increases the probability of plagiarism.

Where there is substantial matched text, the academic has to evaluate the extent to which significant chunks of text are close to or identical to the original source. Such subject experts will recognise any shared language which can be discounted and take into account that there may be limited ways in which some ideas or concepts can be expressed. Eliminating both these categories from the matched items of language will reduce the perceived 'plagiarism' score.

Example 2.1 presents a sample piece of submitted text discussing protection of wildlife. Text matching software highlights the points of similarity using shading to identify the sources (given below the text). This author reordered some paragraphs from one of the original texts and inserted material from other sources, but, in the final analysis, only wrote two original sentences, or, put another way, 50 out of 384 words were written by the person submitting the text. Thus, *verbatim* copying from the original amounted to 87 per cent of the text. Telltale signs of plagiarism in this particular example include the inappropriate brackets round JNCC which may indicate that it was copied and pasted; incorrect syntax in the second sentence of the second paragraph; and the use of an abbreviation, IUCN, indicates that the term had been introduced at an earlier stage – but not in this document.

Example 2.1 Sample text monitored by text matching software. This text shows different parts of the whole text that have been imported from another source without attribution. The legend at the bottom of the text shows different shading corresponding to the actual source of the 'matched text'.

There are a number of organisations with the remit of monitoring the protection of wildlife in the UK. Every five years the statutory nature conservation agencies (Natural England, Countryside Council for Wales and Scottish Natural Heritage) working together through the Joint Nature Conservation Committee (JNCC) are required to review the Wildlife and Countryside Act 1981's Schedules 5 and 8. They then make recommendations to the Secretary of State and Ministers for the Environment based on their review. Schedule 5 lists animals (other than birds) that are specially protected and Schedule 8 lists plants that are specially protected. JNCC is also responsible for the provision of advice on additions to Schedule 9 (non-native species) of the Act.

One of these (JNCC) has an important UK co-ordination role in the provision of advice on species conservation. Advice is delivered mainly through inter-agency groups made up of specialists from Natural England, Scottish Natural Heritage and the Countryside Council conservation. This includes giving advice on UK policy and legislation regarding species, setting up and supporting surveillance and monitoring schemes to assess and report on the changing status of species and carrying out quality assurance assessments of Red Lists, which record species at risk.

Of land species, squirrels are of particular interest as the grey squirrel extends its habitat further and further to the north of the UK prejudicing the habitat and numbers of red squirrels. Experience suggests that, in most areas, it is unlikely that red squirrel populations will persist once the grey squirrel is established. The only exceptions to this may be in very large areas of coniferous forest with few broadleaved trees, though further experimental work is needed to verify this. Any proposed translocation of red squirrels therefore has to be considered very carefully and meet with the IUCN guidelines to maintain a protected species at favourable conservation status. Black squirrels, which originate from North America, were first spotted in Bedfordshire in 1912. They have since been sighted in Hertfordshire and Cambridgeshire.

The UK's habitats are subject to various protective measures. A number of international conventions, European directives and UK laws apply to them, including: The Convention on the Conservation of European Wildlife and Natural Habitats 1979, the Convention on Biological Diversity 1993, the Wildlife and Countryside Act 1981 and the EC Habitats Directive 1992.

Sources:

http://jncc.defra.gov.uk/page-5-theme=textonly

http://jncc.defra.gov.uk/pdf/rs_releaseadvicenote.pdf

http://www.bbc.co.uk/news/uk-england-cambridgeshire-16785217

http://jncc.defra.gov.uk/page-2

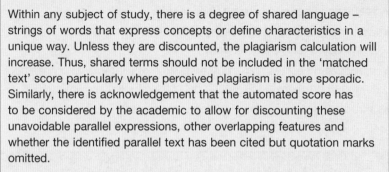

How can I avoid a high 'plagiarism score' when technical terms are unavoidable?

Within any subject of study, there is a degree of shared language – strings of words that express concepts or define characteristics in a unique way. Unless they are discounted, the plagiarism calculation will increase. Thus, shared terms should not be included in the 'matched text' score particularly where perceived plagiarism is more sporadic. Similarly, there is acknowledgement that the automated score has to be considered by the academic to allow for discounting these unavoidable parallel expressions, other overlapping features and whether the identified parallel text has been cited but quotation marks omitted.

Where plagiarism is identified, several possible actions may be taken, such as:

- requiring the student to explain themselves before a disciplinary committee;
- imposing disciplinary measures;
- marking the work down, even to the extent of a zero grade (as would have been the case in Example 2.1); or
- recording the event on the student's transcript (which would be accessible to prospective employers and to the student's professional body – where applicable).

Some examples of text matching software

- *http://safeassign.com*
- *http://www.grammarly.com*
- *http://submit.ac.uk (turnitin uk)*

This by no means a comprehensive list and will change as new products are introduced to the market.

Increasingly, as more and more cases of plagiarism are identified, academics are introducing different modes of engaging students in the process of writing, for example:

- requiring submissions to be handwritten;
- allowing students to accrue credits by submitting work at draft stages before final submission;
- introducing quizzes and 'spot' tests so that students who have not engaged properly in the writing process will be disadvantaged;
- introducing student self- and peer-assessment.

⚙ PRACTICAL TIPS FOR UNDERSTANDING PLAGIARISM

Identify linguistic signatures. Read over different examples of your own work and try to identify phrases or strings of words that you use repeatedly. Do you over-use any expressions, perhaps? These would be what would identify your own 'linguistic signature'. If you were to look at some of your literature sources, you would probably find that you could identify the linguistic signatures of their authors. Thus, linguistic signatures that become intertwined in a single text would indicate very easily to the conscientious reader that some of the text was inconsistent with the remainder. This little exercise in observation could be useful to you in identifying material from sources other than your own that may have been plagiarised.

Identify some examples of 'shared language' in the literature. There will be specialist terms that will be part of the jargon of your subject but there will be other more routine phrases that are used as a matter of course by writers in your field that are devices to address particular aspects of the writing they are producing. A good example can be found particularly in scientific papers: 'Although ..., little is known about xxxx.'

Discuss with friends how plagiarism should be addressed. There are no 'right' answers on these issues, since the reasons for plagiarism may be unknown and diverse. Students who have made 100 per cent effort by producing non-plagiarised work often feel aggrieved when people who have knowingly plagiarised receive better marks. This is a moral issue and debating your opinions on the subject may help to firm up your understanding of what it means to plagiarise and your view on how it should be penalised.

GO AND NOW ...

2.1 Review your time management technique with regard to your writing. As we have seen, plagiarism occurs sometimes because of shortage of time. If you find that you consistently 'run to the wire' in terms of submitting work on time, then it may be useful to consider creating a time-management chart that forces you to be self-disciplined in allocating chunks of time to the different phases of researching, writing and editing. Approach your university's academic support service for some help with your time management strategies.

2.2 Compare academic text with newspaper text. Journalese uses less formal language and a good deal of quotation. Choose any report involving criminal proceedings and work out the percentage of this news that is reported in quotations in the text and its percentage of the whole text. Decide whether this might be inappropriate in academic text.

2.3 Critique subjective writing. Look for statements in a newspaper article that are introduced by unsupported statements such as 'The majority of people...'; 'everyone...'; 'most people ...' and look for any information about the source that provides evidence to support the statement. If you cannot find a newspaper with this kind of language, then listen to oral reporting on news broadcasts and try to identify whether these make unsubstantiated claims in their oral reportage. Look at an academic textbook, periodical or handout and identify whether such statements are used in these.

3

MISCONCEPTIONS ABOUT PLAGIARISM

How to recognise inappropriate use of the work of others

One of the pressures of writing for academic purposes is the emphasis placed on plagiarism as something to be avoided. However, many people are unclear as to what constitutes plagiarism while others believe that simply inserting a reference to source material is sufficient, which is not generally the case. This chapter examines some of the problem issues by scrutinising plagiarism in some of its guises.

KEY TOPICS

→ Plagiarism as an aspect of academic dishonesty – common misconceptions

→ Moving towards successful citation and referencing – knowing the process

KEY TERMS

Academic dishonesty Attribute Bibliography Paraphrasing
Reference list Summarising Synonym

The University of Dundee (2005) provides a simple definition of plagiarism as 'the unacknowledged use of another's work as if it were one's own'. However, the ways in which failure to acknowledge the work of others comes about are various and this can lead to confusion.

PLAGIARISM AS AN ASPECT OF ACADEMIC DISHONESTY – COMMON MISCONCEPTIONS

A number of 'myths' have grown up around the term 'plagiarism'. For example, some people think (wrongly) that plagiarism can be avoided by:

- creating a patchwork of quotations from original text; or
- substituting one or two words with synonyms; or
- re-arranging the wording of the original text; or
- re-ordering the order of sentences; or
- mixing any of the above strategies.

These misconceptions can lead to unintended plagiarism where it appears that the writer has simply not understood the conventions and practices of engaging with the work of others within their own work. However, there is a very thin line between unintended and deliberate plagiarism. Table 3.1 describes several forms of plagiarism, some of which are based on misunderstanding the need for acknowledgement of the source.

In some instances, writers are clearly attempting to take shortcuts to save time or effort and, in the academic world, this is construed as an act of dishonesty or even theft. Example 3.1 provides three examples of alterations to text showing how imported text can dominate a piece of work and that do, therefore, constitute plagiarism of the types described in Table 3.1.

As noted in **Chapter 1**, many writers, especially students, follow the mechanics of punctuation and layout of referencing styles thinking that their job is done. However, Table 3.1 provides examples of where students have failed to conform to the conventions by:

- not giving credit to the source at all;
- including a name–year citation but using exact words from the original without indicating quotation;
- using exact words from the text but without including the source information;
- substituting synonyms with some minor re-ordering of the original text;
- inserting unconnected references randomly and without analysis or rationale;
- downloading text from the internet by cutting and pasting without acknowledgement or date;
- sharing text or work created with another student and not acknowledging the input from the other participant(s); and
- submitting the same piece of work for two different assignments.

Table 3.1 Examples of plagiarism with explanation and suggested corrections. There is often confusion about what constitutes plagiarism. The table shows examples with revisions and explains exactly what the grounds for the plagiarism are. In all cases each would be included in the reference list at the end of the text. Explanation of several points made in the Comments column is given in subsequent chapters.

Category of plagiarism	Example	Revision or suggestion	Comment
Case study 1	Danny has used material direct from the source without any acknowledgement. This is perceived as blatant **plagiarism**.		
Not giving credit to the source at all	*Original:* Most road accidents are alcohol-related: 50% are fatalities but not necessarily of those under alcoholic influence. (Annual Police Statistics 2009 in Milne, 2011) *Danny's text:* The majority of road accidents are alcohol-related and 50% of these cases result in a death but not always of the person who has consumed the alcohol.	*Revision:* A study of police statistics by Milne (2011) reports that approximately half of road accidents result in a death because one of the parties involved has been under the influence of alcohol.	Danny has rearranged the order slightly without noting the source of the data that he cites. This is theft of the original author's intellectual property (IP). Plagiarism aside, he's not explained how these figures were derived and hence they are represented as hearsay rather than hard fact.
Case study 2	Eileen's quoted the exact words from the original text. She has cited the source but has not inserted the quotation marks. However, this is still **plagiarism**.		
Including citation but using words from text without quotation marks	*Original:* It could be assumed that undergraduate students wrote what they could write and not what they actually know. *Eileen's version:* Sim (2006) asserted that students wrote what they could and not what they actually know.	*Revision:* Sim (2006) asserted that students 'wrote what they could and not what they actually know'.	Although Eileen has cited the source, by lifting the exact words taken from the text she is only doing half the job. She must place the exact words within quotation marks (inverted commas).
Case study 3	Ed's copied the words from the original text and placed these within inverted commas but has not sourced the quotes. This, too, is a form of **plagiarism**.		
Using words from text within quotation marks but omitting the citation	*Original:* It could be assumed that undergraduate students wrote what they could write and not what they actually know. *Ed's version:* Essentially, what was noted was that the students 'wrote what they could write and not what they actually know'.	*Revision:* Essentially, it was noted that students 'wrote what they could write and not what they actually know' (Hay, 2010). *Or:* Hay (2010) noted that students 'wrote what they could write and not what they actually know'.	Although he has put in the quotation marks, by not including the source, Ed has failed to give recognition to the intellectual property of Sim. Furthermore, he has failed to understand that the citation brings credibility to his own work.
Case study 4	Xi thinks he can avoid plagiarism by changing odd words and word order of the original text. That is still considered to be **plagiarism**.		
Substituting synonyms with some minor re-ordering of	*Original:* Post-operative physiotherapy is vital to the improvement in the quality of life of the elderly patient (Kay, 2012). *Xi's version:* Therapy after surgery is critical to the recovery	*Revision:* Kay (2012) attributes the improved quality of life levels of elderly patients who have undergone surgery to physiotherapy treatment afterwards.	Xi has used a thesaurus to find synonyms and has reversed two points. This does not show understanding of the issue.

		and picks out the bits she thinks are relevant. She puts those bits that seem to be related together in the same paragraph. Although she puts in the sources and hopes that this evidences her understanding because she has clearly read widely. In reality, the text does not reflect her understanding of the ideas that she is using to illustrate her argument. Thus, this is still **plagiarism**.	
Inserting unconnected references with little linkage or evidence of critical thinking by the student	*Sally's version:* Brown (2000) noted 'insomnia is the ailment of the elderly'. Smith (2004) stated 'insomnia is a function of stressful living'. Jones (2001) said 'insomnia is a figment of those who sleep for an average of 5 hours a night'. This means that insomnia is a problem.	*Revision:* Perceptions about cases of insomnia are varied. Insomnia is problematic for the elderly (Brown, 2000) and the stressed (Smith, 2004). However, Jones (2001) contends that those claiming to be insomniacs actually sleep for an average of 5 hours per night, suggesting that insomnia is often perceived rather than real.	Sally's 'shopping list' of sources fails to make the connection between the explicit point about types of insomniacs and the implicit point that those who claim insomnia do not actually suffer from it. Often students fail to make the underpinning connections or interpretations from the literature to create a substantive discussion of their own.
Case study 6	Jeff has done the prescribed reading and has produced a piece of text that seems slightly too good when compared with the rest of what he has written. The hypertext links suggest that the words are not his own. There is no citation. This is an example of **Internet plagiarism**.		
Downloading from the Internet by cutting and pasting	*Jeff's version:* The incidence of drug misuse is something that invites action from international agencies including the WHO. There are also European organisations that have recognised the need to counter drug trafficking as well as establishing drug rehabilitation regimens throughout the European theatre.	*Revision:* International and European organisations have engaged in tackling drug trafficking, misuse, and rehabilitation. (*www.drugfree.org* accessed 1.1.11)	Jeff's use of this text shows that he has not processed the material. Apart from his reliance on a source that may not be robust in that there is no certainty that his source is monitored or authenticated, he has shown that the has not engaged with the literature from more academic sources.
Case study 7	Marie has worked closely with her student buddy, Tim. They've shared material and both have included the same diagram which is a product of their collaboration. No explanation has been given. This is **plagiarism**.		
'Sharing' (copying?) text *verbatim*/work created with another student	*Marie's version:* Figure 3 shows that … (diagram inserted) *Tim's version:* Figure 3 illustrates that … (diagram inserted)	*Suggested strategy:* It is good to work with a buddy to discuss and sketch the diagram. However, for the final version, both parties should work independently and should acknowledge the contribution of their partner, at an appropriate point, either in the text, the figure legend, the acknowledgements or the reference list.	
Case study 8	Charlie has time management issues – working as a part-time taxi driver and studying between fares – and has not read the regulations to students thoroughly otherwise he would know that he cannot submit the same piece of work twice even if they are for different subjects. In an attempt to keep up with the work, he has handed in two assignments with the different titles but the same content. This is **plagiarism**.		
Handing in the same piece of work for two different assignments	*Charlie's first title:* Economic Consequences of the Barings Bank Collapse (3007 words) *Charlie's second title:* The Kobe Earthquake and Barings Bank (3006 words)	The first titled assignment was submitted for assessment on his Global Economics course. The second title assignment was submitted for assessment on his Business Management course.	There is no way out of this one. With only one word of difference arising from the changed titles, the assignments are duplicates and could easily be identified if processed by text matching software. Both assignments would be zero-rated and would be subject to disciplinary measures.

Example 3.1 Degrees of plagiarism. This box illustrates three instances of plagiarism: (A) shows the original text; the other texts exemplify over-quotation (B), word substitution (C) and re-ordering of original text (D).

A. Original text consists of 51 words.

E-books are a function of the internet era and make access to otherwise unattainable material possible to wider audiences. The globalisation of literature means that individual authors can present their work to a wider audience without incurring abortive publication costs. This facility constitutes a considerable threat to publishers of traditional books.

Source: Watt, W. (2006) *The demise of the book.* Cambridge: The Printing Press (page 13)

B. Plagiarism using too much quotation. This shows a text of 35 words of which 21 words are direct quotation, that is, 60% of the whole text. This is **plagiarism**.

It has been suggested that '**e-books are a function of the internet era**' and that '**globalisation of literature**' allows authors to '**present their work to a wider audience**' without having to incur '**abortive publication costs**' (Watt, 2006).

C.1 Plagiarism overly dependent on word substitution. This shows text where 26 words have been introduced as synonyms or phrases similar in meaning to words used in the original text. This represents 54% of the text being re-worded. This is **plagiarism**.

E-books are part of the internet age and allow many people to use them. This means that writers show their writing from all over the globe on the internet so they do not have such high publicity costs. This feature represents a danger to publishers of old-fashioned books. [*48 words*]

C.2 Original text with word substitutes inserted shown in bold alongside the original wording.

E-books are a function of the internet era (**age**) and make access to otherwise unattainable material possible to wider audiences (**many people**). The globalisation of literature (**from all over the globe**) means that individual authors (**means that writers show**) can present their work to a wider audience without incurring abortive publication costs (**do not have such high publishing costs**). This facility (**feature**) constitutes a considerable threat (**a danger**) to publishers of traditional books (**publishers of old-fashioned books**).

Source: Watt, W. (2006) *The demise of the book.* Cambridge: The Printing Press (page 13)

D. Plagiarism by re-ordering the original sentence sequence. This shows the original text with sentences in a different order and with some phrases moving to other positions and/or sentences. This too is **plagiarism**.

The globalisation of literature is a function of the internet era and means that individual authors can present their work to wider audiences. E-books make access to otherwise unattainable material possible without incurring abortive publication costs which constitutes a considerable threat to publishers of traditional books. [*46 words*]

These examples show that these individuals have a rather shallow understanding of what it means to cite and reference.

> Strategies such as inserting synonyms (words similar in meaning) or changing word or sentence order are regarded as plagiarism. The belief that by altering the text slightly it will escape the notice of the evaluator – human or electronic – is a mistaken one. Word substitution or changes in sentence order do not nullify the plagiarism. As a rule of thumb, between 20 and 50 per cent of identified mis-used text marks it as plagiarised with the subsequent negative results for the author.

MOVING TOWARDS SUCCESSFUL CITATION AND REFERENCING – KNOWING THE PROCESS

Thus, citation and its corresponding referencing is a matter of substance as well as format and involves using the work of others in constructive ways to support your written discussion. This requires some depth of understanding and analytical awareness that includes:

● knowing why you wish to cite one source over another (Table 6.1);
● recognising that citing sources can be done for different purposes, such as to critique a point as well as support a point (**Ch 6**);
● being aware that some of the recognised formats for citing require particular use of language and voice (**Ch 10**) in order to quote, summarise or paraphrase.

Later chapters will provide practical guidance on how to avoid plagiarisin by giving more detailed explanation of the techniques of:

● quoting;
● paraphrasing;
● summarising.

Meantime, the Information box on page 30 gives some useful definitions that will help sort out some of the terms used to refer to different aspects of using the work of others in your own text. This will help you to follow the flowchart in Figure 3.1 more easily (see also **Chapter 1**).

Definitions

Bibliography Dependent on discipline, this can mean either (1) **all** the literature read on a subject but not necessarily cited in the text or (2) **only** the literature cited in the text.

Citation The publication detail given in the text that identifies the original source of the information being given as well as the content included by integrating quotation or paraphrased texts.

Quotation The use of words taken directly from the text produced by another author and identified by using the punctuation conventions of quotation marks or indentation where a quotation is more than 30 words drawn from the original text.

Paraphrasing Restating the key ideas of a text, giving sense, idea or meaning in other words, but in more detail than in summarising.

Reference list The list of all sources cited in the text providing all necessary bibliographical information that would enable the reader to source the original document.

Referencing style For the purposes of this book, the term 'style' is used to identify the different formats that are used for the purposes of citation and referencing. You may also see these called 'methods' or 'guides' in other publications.

Summarising Creating a broad overview of an original piece of text, briefly stating the main idea but using your own words, giving less detail than in paraphrasing.

Figure 3.1 shows the notional steps to follow in moving from the first stages of thinking about a new topic through to the final content of the draft text. This may be helpful in helping you to map out what you need to think about with regard to the purpose of alluding to the work of others in your own text. It is photocopiable and so you may wish to use it as a checklist to help go through the process in the earlier stages.

 PRACTICAL TIPS FOR DEVELOPING UNDERSTANDING IN ACADEMIC TEXTS

Check the meanings of words. The key terms sections at the beginning of each of the chapters in this book relate to words used within the chapter that have been identified as ones that may be less

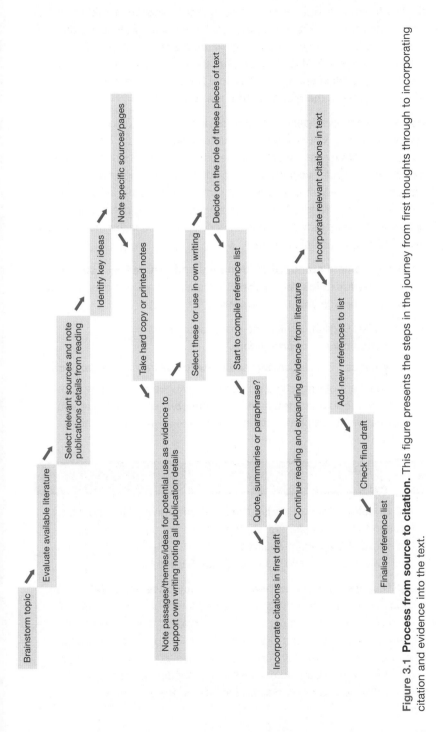

Figure 3.1 Process from source to citation. This figure presents the steps in the journey from first thoughts through to incorporating citation and evidence into the text.

familiar to you. Take a moment to consult the Glossary section at the end of the book to ensure that your understanding of these words is accurate because sometimes words have different meanings in different contexts. In this chapter, perhaps the word 'synonym' is a word that you have encountered before but cannot remember the meaning. Confirm the meaning from the Glossary.

Use standard and specialist dictionaries. When reading around your subject area, you will probably encounter words that are either new to you or familiar words that seem to be used in new contexts. You can expand your regular vocabulary by looking up these new words in a standard dictionary or in a specialist dictionary if the terms are specific to your subject. Standard dictionaries are available in public and university libraries as well as online; specialist dictionaries may only be available in your university library.

Bookmark online standard dictionaries and also subject specific dictionaries for quick reference. Good standard online dictionaries may be available through your library website.

- For British English, it might be worth bookmarking *www.macmillandictionary.com*.
- For American English, *nws.merriam-webster.com/opendictionary*.
- For speakers of English as an additional language, you may find it useful to bookmark *www.ldoceonline.com* which will give you information about pronunciation and usage as well as meaning.

(GO) AND NOW ...

3.1 Check a piece of earlier text that you have authored. Read through the text to identify whether you have committed any of the errors of plagiarism outlined in Table 3.1. Reflect on what you might have done to avoid any errors of that type.

3.2 Discuss with some friends what they understand by plagiarism. After reading this chapter you should be more aware of what constitutes plagiarism. However, since there is much misunderstanding about this, it may help you to identify how some impressions may be inaccurate. Sometimes explaining something to someone else can aid our own understanding by clarifying thoughts and this could well be the case in this instance.

3.3 Look briefly at the citation styles modelled in Part 5 – Five Referencing Styles. Different subjects/courses on your study programme or publications for which you may write may require you to follow different citation styles. You will also need to be able to recognise different styles used in the source material that you read and to amend it accordingly to follow the guidelines required for a particular text. Skim over **Chs 11–15** to see if any of them are familiar to you and whether you can identify the format used in your own discipline.

4

BASICS OF LITERATURE SEARCHING

How to be aware of the sources of literature

When you set out to produce a serious piece of academic writing, you will have a definite purpose. For example, you may need to write an essay, a report, a literature review, a dissertation, a thesis, an article for publication in an academic journal or a chapter for a book. Each type of task requires a different stylistic approach. The first thinking stages in the research process will be broadly similar and will require initial stages of research and reading to construct a framework for your understanding. Your work will benefit from a sound appreciation of this process.

KEY TOPICS

→ First steps in researching the literature

→ Appraising content in the literature

→ Reaching an opinion about the reliability of the literature

→ Tracking the development of your understanding

→ Using technology for organising citations and references

KEY TERMS

Abstract *Caveat* Conjecture Encyclopaedia Indices Nuance
Peer review Primary source Provenance Secondary source
Triangulation Value judgement

At the beginning of any project – regardless of your level or experience – the initial step is to find your way into the literature to gain a basic understanding of the context. Gradually, you will find more detailed resource material that might, for example, address some of the contemporary debate or problem issues relating to your topic. Along the way, you will find that key concepts begin to emerge and that certain names recur in the literature. All of this gives you the in-depth knowledge backed by evidence from the literature to support your own particular perspective on the topic.

FIRST STEPS IN RESEARCHING THE LITERATURE

- **Brainstorming your own ideas.** Before you begin foraging for literature it is a good idea to brainstorm your initial thoughts on the subject. This is a way of ensuring that you avoid inadvertently using the work of others without acknowledgement. By brainstorming your topic, you have a record of your own first thoughts and hence ownership of these. This helps you begin the process of researching and evaluating the literature. In addition, this initial brainstorm will help you to analyse the task that you have been set or, where none has been set, help you to define the parameters of your analysis. Figure 3.1 lays out the steps in that process so that you can understand what the endpoint is and so work towards it. An example of a brainstorm is provided in **Chapter 9**.

- **Becoming familiar with the techniques of searching.** Initial work will involve reading around the subject in order to expand your understanding of the wider field and then becoming more selective in the types of specific source material you consult. You need to develop an awareness of specialist search engines and specialist journals to help you to find material relevant for your work and to broaden your understanding of your topic.

Using your librarian's expertise

If you are using a library that is new to you or if you are embarking on a new area of study, for example, then it is important to identify the specialist sources that might be available in your library. Library websites, for example, may provide specialist portals that provide information about resources for specific disciplines. In addition, there may be a librarian with a particular remit to cover that area. You can consult them in person or go on a brief library training course to find out more, developing what librarians call 'information literacy', especially your research techniques. Becoming aware of specialist search engines and specialist journals will help you to find material for your work and broaden your understanding of your topic.

- **Becoming familiar with the literature.** Your list of recommended reading will guide you in your search for relevant material; If you don't have such a list, you will need to start your research of the literature from first principles. The stage that you are in your studies will dictate what is expected of you and the material you consult. For example, textbook sources may be more appropriate to initial and earlier levels of undergraduate study rather than specialist periodical sources used by more advanced students. If you are an experienced researcher or academic, then you will already have a fairly detailed knowledge of the available journal sources. Typical categories of resources that you might consult are listed in Table 4.1.

✔ Effective searching

When you are researching for material, be aware of different spelling conventions since you might spell a word in a way that yields no titles, but if you spell it in another way, you may find a wealth of resources. You should be aware particularly of:

- differences in spellings of family names e.g. Macmillan and McMillan; Smith and Smyth;

- differences between British English spellings and American English spellings, e.g. organization and organisation; practise (verb) and practice (noun) (British English) and practise (both noun and verb in American English);

- international standards for certain professional expressions e.g. sulfur (American Scientific English) and the British spelling of sulphur. The former is the accepted professional norm;

- different parts of speech that might be used in titles e.g. organisation(noun)/organise(verb);

- different 'labels' e.g. **Political Science** possibly equates with **Politics**, therefore you should search under both;

- difference in language e.g. escuela (Spanish for 'school') and school where the similarity is not a problem; however, 'periódico' (Spanish for 'newspaper') should not be confused with periodical in the sense of an academic journal and;

- use of acronyms (NATO, WHO, UNICEF) which are famous in their own right and have entered the language, but to source a fuller vein of resources you might need to search under **N**orth **A**tlantic **T**reaty **O**rganisation, **W**orld **H**ealth **O**rganisation and **U**nited **N**ations **I**nternational **C**hildren's **E**ducation **F**und.

Table 4.1 Types of resource. Positive and negative aspects of these resources are listed.

Reference resources provide an overview or specific factual information; some subject-specific.	
✓ **Encyclopaedias:** Some provide brief entries, others give highly detailed information, often with links to related items and with reference list supporting an entry. ✓ **Dictionaries:** online or hard copy can provide general word meanings and pronunciation; specialist dictionaries offer meanings and particular usage of specialist terms.	✗ The level of detail depends on the type of encyclopaedia being consulted. ✗ Hard copy encyclopaedias can become out-of-date quite quickly. ✗ Caution advised when using 'free content' style online encyclopaedias since there may be no moderation to ensure accuracy.
Textbooks may be prescribed texts.	
✓ Provide general contextual background and coverage relating to the course content. ✓ Supplementary textbooks may provide in-depth more specialist coverage.	✗ Can become out-of-date quite quickly. ✗ Heavy to carry. ✗ Difficult to access if library availability is limited.
Academic journals and periodicals. Produced two to four times a year. Often available online via academic libraries with subscriptions; allows access for own academic community.	
✓ Articles in these publications are usually written by subject specialists for an academic discipline-specific readership. ✓ In traditional journals, articles are 'peer reviewed' which means that the content is evaluated by an expert in the field who makes a recommendation to accept or reject the article for publication. ✓ Some libraries may hold bound copies of archived journals that pre-date the online versions.	✗ Some are more credible than others – e.g. the *British Medical Journal* (BMJ) has greater prestige than non-refereed online journals that have no quality control. ✗ Need to verify the quality of the journal consulted. An elegant web page alone does not authenticate its content. ✗ To judge quality, look at the names listed as the editorial board and also identify whether the web page is hosted by an academic institution or other organisation.
Grey (gray) literature. Term used in library and information science to describe materials, print and electronic, produced by organisations outside recognised commercial publishing houses – e.g. relating to government, academia, business and industry. Examples might include White Papers, technical reports or in-house publications and can be primary sources in some subjects.	
✓ Interpretations evolving as technology provides non-professional publication possibilities	✗ Random creation makes tracking difficult. ✗ Authorship is difficult to identify. ✗ Transience; may lack formal archive. ✗ Origins may be outside the 'establishment' and be part of an underground movement. ✗ Lack of bibliographical information makes it difficult to create a conventional citation.
Media. Newspapers, television or radio that present information to wide audiences.	
✓ Provide contemporary and even 'real time' information and coverage of topical issues ✓ Offer commentary on current issues	✗ Questionable objectivity used by such media; some favour particular political viewpoints and are written by journalists for sensationalist and populist ends. ✗ In several disciplines the use of material from the media would be unacceptable.

- **Using an encyclopaedia as a starting guide for additional research sources.** Standard well-researched encyclopaedias – hard copy or their online versions – not only provide a broad overview of a topic but also include a useful list of references that will help you to extend your search for more detailed material. These references are usually given at the end of an entry and will be presented in one of the conventional referencing styles. The online versions offer a considerable degree of functionality with hypertext links and the ability to search for related items. However, an element of caution should be acknowledged in relation to such resources where the provenance is less certain. For example, the examples shown in Table 4.2 demonstrate the difference in style and approach to providing information between an online 'traditional' encyclopaedia and an online 'free content and openly editable' encyclopaedia.

- **Specialist encyclopaedias and dictionaries.** These exist for many disciplines, sometimes comprehensive in their inclusion of material that might cover a wide range of subject areas, whereas others are highly specialised. These are useful in that they can provide a 'broad brush' approach to a subject written by an expert that can resolve lack of understanding or confirm terms or facts, for example.

i

Health warning on wiki-style encyclopaedias

The entries in standard hard-copy encyclopaedias and their online equivalents are compiled by recognised experts in the field. Hence, they are well-researched, authoritative and reliably attributed to the authors and sources from which they have been drawn for the encyclopaedia entry. However, some free access online encyclopaedias – wiki-style resources – are comprised of entries created by their readership. In some instances contributions are made by subject experts, but others are not necessarily made by people of expertise. Quality varies. In some instances, references are provided, in others not. This means that the information may – or may not – have been refereed or evaluated for accuracy, impartiality or currency. Sometimes this lack of verification is flagged up on the site. Thus, you should be cautious and not regard material from such online journals as reliable or up to the standard that you will need for your research. Always check in other more impeccable sources before you incorporate the information into your own work.

Table 4.2 Online encyclopaedias. Both entries are responses to the research term 'plebiscite' and demonstrate differences in accuracy, depth and style. Underlining indicates hypertext links.

Encyclopaedia Britannica online	Wikipedia online
Plebiscite	A **referendum** (also known as a **plebiscite** or a vote on a **ballot question**) is a direct vote in which an entire electorate is asked to either accept or reject a particular proposal. This may result in the adoption of a new constitution, a constitutional amendment, a law, the recall of an elected official or simply a specific government policy. It is a form of direct democracy. The word *plebiscite* comes from the Latin *plebiscita*, which originally meant a decree of the *Concilium Plebis*, the popular assembly of the Roman Republic. *Referendums* and *referenda* are both commonly used as plurals of *referendum*. [*102 words*]
Plebiscites are elections held to decide two paramount types of political issues: government legitimacy and the nationality of territories contested between governments. In the former case, the incumbent government, seeking a popular mandate as a basis for legitimacy, employs a **plebiscite** to establish its right to speak for the nation. **Plebiscites** of this nature are thought to establish a direct link between the rulers and the ruled; intermediaries such as political parties are bypassed, and for this reason **plebiscites** are sometimes considered antithetical to pluralism and competitive politics. Following the **French Revolution** in 1789, the **plebiscite** was widely popular … [*100 words*]	
	Source: http://en.wikipedia.org/wiki/ Referendum (Accessed 17.2.12)
Source: http://www.britannica.com/ EBchecked/topic/182308/election/229019/ Plebiscite (Accessed 17.2.12)	This entry gives an explanation that is more about application rather than theoretical analysis. The fact that 'plebiscite' is given as a synonym for 'referendum' shows that this resource does not always give such fine-grained information as more formal resources which explore different nuances of meaning.
This entry gives an explanation which might be regarded as more 'purist' in format and content.	

- **Using reviews in initial research.** In the sciences, especially, a supervisor may set a topic for a student to review as an introduction to a field. In these instances, 'Annual Reviews in …' series would provide a good starting point. Another useful resource might be the 'mini-reviews' that are often positioned at the front of journals. These resources have the advantage of being more current than perhaps the course textbook.

APPRAISING CONTENT IN THE LITERATURE

Academic material will offer you a wide variety of facts and ideas originating from research and scholarship. Descriptions, concepts and interpretations of numerical data contribute to the published material you will read. This may take the form of textbooks based on many years of study in an area or, as part of the process of advancing research, be published academic journals. However, not everything that you find in the literature relating to your topic will necessarily offer the quality of evidence that you need. Indeed, some literature may be best avoided for a number of reasons – unreliability of content, dubiety about its authorship or even plagiarism. Therefore, establishing the provenance (a word that embraces both origin and implied quality) is important in evaluating the soundness of the content of each piece of literature you consider. Table 4.3 provides a checklist that will lead you to be able to reach a judgement about the validity of the sources you find.

Table 4.3 **A checklist for assessing the reliability of information.** These questions are based on commonly adopted criteria; the more 'yes' answers you can give, the more trustworthy you can assume your source to be.

Assessing authorship and the nature of the source	Evaluating the information and its analysis
❑ Can you identify the author's name?	❑ Is the source cited by others?
❑ Can you determine what relevant qualifications they hold?	❑ Is the date of the source likely to be important regarding the accuracy of the information? For example, is it contemporary to events, or is it written with the benefit of hindsight?
❑ Can you say who employs the author?	❑ Have you focused on the substance of the information presented rather than its packaging?
❑ Do you know who paid for the work to be done? For example, a petrol company paying for research into oil spillage would have a particular interest in achieving a specific viewpoint.	❑ Is the information fact or opinion?
❑ Is this a primary source rather than a secondary one?	❑ Have you checked for any logical fallacies in the arguments?
❑ Has the source been refereed or edited?	❑ Does the language used indicate anything about the status of the information?
❑ Is the content original or derived?	❑ Have the errors associated with any numbers been taken into account?
❑ Does the source cite relevant literature?	❑ Have the data been analysed using appropriate statistics?
❑ Have you checked a range of sources?	❑ Are any graphs constructed fairly?

In order to develop some confidence in the material you are reading, you will also have to appraise it for reliability and quality of research. A number of factors have to be taken into account in this respect. These include:

- **Authorship.** If you have done even a small amount of reading, you should be able to identify whether an author has a reputation in the area by using a search engine. For example, you may identify whether that author is entirely 'self-published' and so perhaps is lacking in academic research credentials or whether their work has been recognised in high impact journals. They may even be considered an authority in the field.

- **Provenance.** This is the word used to describe the chronological thread of published research and other sources. The provenance of academic writing (the 'history' of its authorship and publication) is important because it helps establish whether it is based on sound research principles or is simply unsupported or weakly supported opinion. An additional factor that may influence your perception of the provenance is to identify whether the material is a primary or a secondary source. This is explained more fully in the Information box overleaf.

- **Repeatability.** In the natural and formal sciences as well as in the arts and social sciences, one interpretation of reliability is that the observation or experiment could be repeated by a competent peer to launch a new thread of investigation, for example. The track record and authority of the person making the assertion, or the nature of the evidence which is cited to support a case will encourage confidence in the research reported.

- **Peer reviewed publication.** This is where the material is reviewed by one or more academics ('referees') working in the same field – hence, peer review. This is done by journals before an item is accepted for publication. This helps to ensure:
  - originality of the material;
  - maintenance of the standards of the publication;
  - citation of all relevant past work;
  - due consideration of conflicting theories and opinions;
  - accuracy in any data and calculations; and
  - validity of interpretations of information and data.

Characteristics and examples of primary and secondary sources of information

Primary sources: those in which ideas and data are first communicated.

■ The primary literature in your subject may be published in the form of papers (articles) in journals.

■ The primary literature is usually refereed by experts in the authors' academic peer group, who check the accuracy and originality of the work and report their opinions back to the journal editors. This system is called 'peer reviewing' and, although it is not perfect, it helps maintain reliability.

■ Books (and, more rarely, articles in magazines and newspapers) can also be primary sources, but this depends on the nature of the information published rather than the medium. These sources are not formally refereed, although they may be read by editors and lawyers to check for errors and unsubstantiated or libellous allegations.

Secondary sources: those that quote, adapt, interpret, translate, develop or otherwise use information drawn from primary sources.

■ It is the act of recycling that makes the sources secondary, rather than the medium. Reviews are examples of secondary sources in the academic world, and textbooks and magazines are often of this type.

■ As people adopt, modify, translate and develop information and ideas, alterations are likely to occur, whether intentional or unintentional. Most authors of secondary sources do not deliberately set out to change the meaning of the primary source, but they may unwittingly do so. Others may consciously or unconsciously exert bias in their reporting by quoting evidence on one side of a debate.

■ Modifications while creating a secondary source could involve adding valuable new ideas and content, or correcting errors.

● **Discrimination of fact, opinion and conjecture.** Being aware of the differences that arise in considering fact, opinion and conjecture is key to evaluating academic text. The most basic kinds of facts are those that are 'common knowledge', for example, that *'the capital of Italy is Rome'*. Other facts might be more specific but less well-known, for example, that *'this book is published by Pearson'* is a fact. Similarly, in the academic world, facts are used as starting points for examining evidence. In the natural and formal sciences facts may be less well-known or acknowledged outside the field but are robustly acknowledged within it. In the social sciences facts also play a role. For example, *'Rome sits on the River Tiber'* is a fact that might be stated by a geographer, and represents an undisputed fact. However, there is often no 'right' or 'wrong' answer about issues considered in these disciplines, simply a range of viewpoints with supporting evidence. Thus, these are not 'facts' but views or opinions. These may be represented arising out of laboratory, field or literature research and subsequent interpretation of the evidence. However, academics often drive their research forward by embarking on journeys of conjecture. In these cases, a range of conditions are imagined and the possible consequences are analysed. Their conjectures start with 'what if ...?' questions and can build up into a line of enquiry that will develop an area further than the established wisdom might have suggested.

- **Recognising value judgements.** Poor writing based on the opinions of the writer which 'lead' the reader to follow the view of the writer whose statements are without evidential substance can be made so assertively that they project an image of certainty that is unfounded. Hence, you need to be vigilant if you come across expressions such as *'everyone knows that ...'*, *'the majority view is that ...'* (without any supporting data) or *'clearly, there is no support for this'* (without drawing on data to justify the use of the 'absolute' word 'no'). Often such statements are based on hearsay and have a tendency to reflect subjectivity or bias. The term 'value judgement' is explained in the Glossary.

REACHING AN OPINION ABOUT THE RELIABILITY OF THE LITERATURE

In order to obtain ideas and evidence for your own writing, you will be considering complex ideas and views in the content of the literature. To help you come to an opinion regarding a particular resource, you will need to:

- read any summary or abstract that relates to the document (if any) to gain a broad overview of the content;
- read and understand the source material in full;
- check facts and assertions that are made by the author;

- judge the issues that are raised on the basis of data or other evidence given; and

- decide how far you agree or disagree with the views expressed in the source.

By taking all these factors into account in selecting and then reading source content you can then expand your own view or understanding, so that you can decide whether you are going to incorporate the idea(s) or viewpoint(s) in your own writing and for what purpose. For example, you may wish to endorse, emphasise or reject points in your discussion.

TRACKING THE DEVELOPMENT OF YOUR UNDERSTANDING

As already noted, when you read, you will gradually identify key themes and concepts and begin to link them to particular thinkers, researchers and authors who have contributed to the area that you

i Abstracts in periodical and journal articles as research resources

An abstract or summary is usually found at the beginning of the paper. They provide a useful outline of the aims and outcomes in research, providing a quick overview of the topic since it gives key information on the methods, ideas and conclusions discussed in the text. This has two points of importance for the researcher:

- the abstract can indicate whether it is worth spending time on reading the whole text for deeper analysis and evaluation of the evidence provided;

- the abstract can make claims that a critical reader might question and this would prompt checking of the full article to evaluate results or conclusions that may be dubious.

These abstracts are often collated into academic indices (plural of index) or online databases to assist researchers in identifying whether the full paper is going to be relevant to their research purpose.
Note that, if you find an abstract that seems to be relevant, in most disciplines it is expected that you will consult the full article to evaluate its merits and demerits; you cannot simply cite the abstract.

are examining. As a consequence you will build up an overview of some of the facts, opinions and conjectures that they have expressed in their writing. In this process, there is potential for the blurring of ownership of ideas as you assimilate information and broaden your own understanding. This can be a critical stage on the pathway to plagiarism, both intentional and unintentional. Unless you take deliberate steps to note down the publication details of your sources to use when creating a citation, then there is a danger that you might subsume points into your own writing without acknowledging the original source.

USING TECHNOLOGY FOR ORGANISING CITATIONS AND REFERENCES

Reference management software (RMS) packages have been developed to allow automatic recording of citations and their corresponding entries into the reference list usually found at the end of an academic text. In some situations in higher education, use of such a package is mandatory, but more often the choice is up to the writer.

There are a number of RMS packages available and your decision to use this kind of software would have to take account of whether:

● the RMS is compatible with the word processing package that you are using;

● the RMS is capable of file exchange with users of another RMS system, if applicable to your need;

● a cost is involved or whether use of the RMS is free;

? What publication information do I need to note down?

Some commercial electronic referencing software packages offer as many as 200 choices of citation and referencing style which presents a confusing array of possibilities. Part 2 of this book provides samples of the ones most commonly used in UK universities and demonstrates the mechanics of layout for citations within the text and formats for the reference list presented at the end of a text. However, in the early stages of researching your topic, it is necessary only to concentrate on the information that would be required for most forms of citation and referencing.

For most citation and referencing systems what you will need to record is the following:

■ **Who?**	Full **name of author** – include all authors if more than one	Surname, first name or initials
■ **What?**	Full **title**	For example, book title, journal article, chapter (and book title), broadcast programme or film title (and edition, if known)
■ **When?**	**Date** of publication/ broadcast	Normally shown in the back of the title page along with the ISBN reference. Note date at time of broadcast
■ **Where?**	**Place** of publication	Normally shown in the back of the title page along with the ISBN reference
■ **By whom?**	**Publisher** or **journal**	Normally shown in the back of the title page along with the ISBN reference
■ **Chapter/page numbers**	**Pages** of the full article or chapter	You may need to return to the source document to check up on a phrase or section that you intend to cite. Knowing the precise pages will help save time.

- the RMS is intuitively user-friendly or it will require a considerable investment of time to learn how to use it efficiently. For example, one user manual consists of 680 pages to be digested in order to use the functions fully which suggests that the effort may not match any benefit in time-saving;

- the time spent learning how to use the RMS is going to pay time-saving dividends or whether a simpler manual version of organising references as a table or spreadsheet may be sufficient for your need.

Advantages of RMS packages are that:

- Citation information can be inserted in the text consistently following the conventions of a selected citation style.

- Each in-text citation is matched to the corresponding publication details in the reference list.

- Full publication details need only be typed once.

- A database is created consisting of a large number of references from which a selection can be made for other publication purposes.

- One citation style should, in theory, be able to be converted to another style using RMS functions.

Yet, there are serious *caveats* about the use of RMS tools, namely, that they simply deal with the mechanical aspects of layout. The responsibility for selecting source material, evaluating its merits and incorporating it into the wording of the writer's text remains with the writer. While the RMS might save time in some respects, the information data still need to be keyed into the RMS database so some of the chore remains even when using the technology. For undergraduates, especially, the merit of spending considerable amounts of time learning how to use the software could be questionable. However, the decision remains with the writer.

Further information on the functionality and relative merits of some of the more commonly used RMS packages can be found in a useful table at: ***https://workspace.imperial.ac.uk/library/Public/Reference_management_software_comparison.pdf***. Note that university libraries and information technology centres often provide training courses on use of RMS packages.

Plan in advance. Sometimes there will be heavy demand for texts that have been recommended by lecturers. If that is the case, ensure that you have arranged to reserve the publication or have booked a time to consult the reference in your library.

Be critical in your reading. Just because something has been printed does not make it valid; just because someone with a reputation in an area asserts an opinion, this does not mean that it is 'right'. Hence, in your reading, you should be prepared to look for flaws in the logic of argument, weak evidence or incorrect facts and be prepared to challenge with counter-argument, conflicting evidence or verified facts.

Be systematic in your reading and recording publication data. When selecting source material, record publication details of everything you read on the topic. This is important because you may find that points dismissed in the early stages of your reading may emerge as more significant and you will save yourself time if you can quickly refer back to the list of publications you read earlier. Note also that it is sometimes difficult to ascertain authorship for online publications. It is important not to ignore these, but you may need to be more inventive in establishing the details. One tactic would be to look for clues in the header, body and footer information on-screen.

Be aware of fact, opinion and conjecture. When you are reading academic texts, you must be alert to what has been said that is undisputed fact, what is the opinion of the writer based on evidence they have presented or what is their conjecture arising out of a set of circumstances that remain hypothetical, or put more colloquially, guesswork. You can evaluate the worth of these writings by 'triangulation' of one author's views with those of others by consulting and comparing different sources that address the same or similar issues.

Be systematic in your note-making. Some people prefer to make notes as they read, although it is arguably more efficient to read first and then compile notes. It is also a good idea to note the date on which you did the reading/made the notes and, of course, the publication details should be recorded on your notes so that you have all the essential details for the reference list. Thorough guidelines on making notes effectively can be found in McMillan and Weyers (2012).

4.1 Identify and browse specialist encyclopaedias. For some disciplines there are specialist encyclopaedias (and dictionaries) that you should investigate. These could provide you with quick and reliable baseline information about diverse aspects of your discipline. These usually go beyond the level of information given in generic encyclopaedias and dictionaries.

4.2 Identify available periodicals in your subject area. Since web access has made periodicals (journals) easily available to all, there needs to be a word of caution regarding their use. Periodicals are generally more appropriate to the work of researchers, postgraduates and senior undergraduates. These publications are written by specialists for specialists; less experienced writers can become bogged down in the detail and jargon. The more fundamental appraisal provided in textbook reading can provide more basic understanding which may be all that is necessary, depending on the level of study. That said, knowing the key periodicals in your area can be useful because the articles in them can provide the framework for understanding of the wider field. Listen for references to periodicals or journals that might be made in lectures, but be aware that they may only be accessible through subscription. If your library does not include a particular journal in its portfolio of subscriptions, then this will not be available to you.

4.3 Organise your list of references as you read. In your reading, you may not realise whether a particular point will be used in your work or not. It is often useful to set up a temporary reference list of all the sources that you have read. In this way, should you discover that something that you read but from which you did not necessarily take notes is going to be required, then you can source the document more quickly.

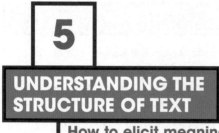

5

UNDERSTANDING THE STRUCTURE OF TEXT

How to elicit meaning in material for potential citation

Your first thoughts outlined in your initial brainstorm will be supplemented by ideas you've read about and your reflections on these. As your understanding deepens, you will begin to select particular points in your source material that could possibly be incorporated into your discussion. In this way you will begin to be clearer about how you will construct your own text and your thinking will develop further as you write.

KEY TOPICS

→ Models of approach in structuring academic text

→ Selecting sources for citation

KEY TERMS

Function   Reflection   Refuting   Seminal literature   Value judgement   *verbatim*

When selecting an idea that you wish to integrate into your own work, there are four key questions that you need to ask yourself with regard to the original source text:

1 **What part** of the text will you use? – Which part or parts of the text best reflect the idea you wish to cite?

2 **By whom** was it written? – Who was the author (+ name of publication)

3 **When** was it written?

   – Date of publication – is this a recent piece of work or is it still valid and contemporary?

   – Is the date important to your appraisal of the literature and your current purpose?

4 **Why** do you wish to include this? – What *function* (or purpose) will this particular citation perform in your own writing? For example, will this point be in support of the case you are making or does it represent a counter-argument?

Points 1 to 4 were covered in **Chapter 4**; this current chapter examines the fourth question about the types of judgements you may need to make when selecting the ideas you wish to include as particular text references within your work. This involves understanding the range of models that you might adopt in constructing your text.

Noting page numbers for future reference

In the initial stages, when you are noting *verbatim* text, you may not know whether you are going to quote or paraphrase the content. Therefore, in addition to noting all the publication details, it is worth noting the page number of the selected text so that you have that information to hand if you decide to present this as a *quotation* within your own writing as you will need to provide page numbers so that readers, if they wish, could consult the original source.

MODELS OF APPROACH IN STRUCTURING ACADEMIC TEXT

The nature of academic writing often follows particular patterns depending on the purpose of the writing and the level of study. However, although this can be a matter of scale, the principles are the same. Seven of the most common models of constructing academic text are shown in Table 5.1.

Within their writing, even within the same text, writers may adopt different approaches. For example, in order to conduct an objective analysis, the writer may adopt the situation-problem-solution-evaluation-recommendation model (or SPSER) (Table 5.1). Table 5.2 shows in greater detail how the writer can construct a case step-by-step, all while considering different aspects of the issue or situation being analysed. In this particular example, this involves the writer in describing a process, presenting positive and negative aspects, stating an opinion and giving reasons in support of that opinion. These aspects of the text are known in language terms as 'functions'; in

Table 5.1 Seven of the most common structural models used in academic writing. These models are explained in greater detail in McMillan and Weyers (2012).

Type of model	Definition
1 Chronological	Describing a process or sequence
2 Classifying	Ordering objects or ideas
3 Common denominator	Identifying a common characteristic or theme
4 Phased	Identifying short/medium/long-term aspects
5 Analytical	Examining an issue in depth by considering a situation, the problem within it, solution(s), evaluation of the solution(s) and possibly a recommendation (See Table 5.2)
6 Thematic	Commenting on a theme in each aspect of the work
7 Comparative/ contrastive	Comparing and contrasting (often within a theme or themes)

Table 5.2 How writing within the analytical (SPSER) model relates to functions. This framework provides a good basis for organising writing, particularly where the issues are complex. It encourages a methodical approach that can help the underlying thinking that goes on even in the process of writing itself.

1 Situation	• **Describing** the context perhaps in a chronological way or by themes or, in the research case, by outlining the seminal literature. This simply reports what the situation involves *without expressing any opinion*.
2 Problem	• **Describing** the problem as the writer perceives it, based on evidence available. Sometimes this will involve: – **presenting supporting evidence** and/or – **presenting contradictory evidence**. At this stage, normally no opinion is expressed.
3 Solution(s)	• **Describing a possible solution or solutions.**
4 Evaluation of solution(s)	• **Giving reasons for favouring** each solution possibly by providing evidence from the literature or from data. • **Giving reasons for refuting (rejecting)** each solution possibly by providing evidence from the literature or from data.
5 Recommendation	• **Stating an opinion.** • **Giving reasons for that opinion** possibly by providing evidence from the literature or from data.

well-written text, it should be possible to identify the 'function' in each paragraph. They are the underpinning constructs of extended writing formats such as those required at higher academic levels. This is a useful concept in both analysing reading and in framing your own writing. Table 5.3 shows some examples of functions that may be used to incorporate citations as part of the discussion within academic texts.

Table 5.3 Examples of roles citations perform in academic writing. Citation of the work of others is fundamental to academic writing; this can be included in the introduction where existing literature is reviewed or later in the work, for example, to explain theoretical approaches or interpretation within the conclusion of a report style text. They would appear throughout a literature review.

Role in discussion	Function	Action
Examining existing literature	Reporting/describing	• Outlining work done to date chronologically
	Reporting/describing	• Outlining work done to date thematically
	Exemplifying	• Giving examples
	Classifying	• Grouping aspects into categories or themes
	Justifying	• Explaining reasons for development of work thus far
Presenting a viewpoint	Asserting	• Stating a viewpoint
	Observing	• Acknowledging a piece of information
	Making a claim	• Proposing an idea/position
	Justifying	• Presenting evidence in support
	Surmising	• Suggesting a possible theory or consequence
Structuring an analysis or argument	Evaluating	• Presenting positive views in favour of a position
	Contradicting/ Refuting	• Presenting counter-arguments or views
	Endorsing	• Showing agreement with a viewpoint
Comparing and contrasting approaches	Critiquing work	• Considering strengths • Considering weaknesses
Cause and effect relationships	Identifying relationships	• Explaining the reasons that result in particular situations or conditions

SELECTING SOURCES FOR CITATION

To demonstrate why some sections of text might be rejected while others are selected, it may be helpful to look at a practical example. Table 5.4 shows the relationship between the content and the intended function within a text, but balances this against the quality of the content. Table 5.5 shows 12 examples of quotations with their corresponding functions. The information in the quotation might be used to support the discussion in the text. Quotation, summarising and paraphrasing are covered in **Chapter 7** and **Chapter 8**.

Table 5.4 Rejecting content from selected source material. For ease of reference, the original quotation form has been adopted; the intention would be to paraphrase for citation purposes. Some ideas (column 3) were rejected because they were based on value judgements which are often indicative of sloppy writing that does not support the view proposed with hard evidence.

Original text	Function	Reason for rejection
1 Disadvantage of wind power So-called 'wind farms' blight the landscape and give a return that is disproportionate to investment and the space that they take up. (Watt, J. 2009. *The Eye of the Storm.* London: Windmill Press)	Stating opinion	✗ Not used Subjective Value judgement Not relevant to purpose
2 Advantages of wind power Windmills provide enough energy to fuel a significant UK town and they are perceived to add to tourist interest in an area. (Breeze, A. 2007. *The New Tomorrow.* York: Netherworld Press)	Supporting opinion	✗ Not used No supporting evidence
3 Advantages of wind-farm technology After development work, the modern wind turbine has low cost maintenance that reflects the reliability of the product. (*Free Energy Marketing Journal*, 2010, vol. 3.2, 19–23)	Reporting fact Expressing opinion	✗ Not used No supporting data Value judgement
4 The farming community and wind technology Traditional farmers will not be directly affected by the revolution in technology since wind farms are largely positioned in uncultivated areas of the country. (*Wind Farming Journal*, 2011, vol. 1, 56–73)	Expressing opinion	✗ Not used Not relevant Not supported by data

Table 5.5 Selecting relevant text based on function required to construct discussion. Again, for ease of understanding, the original quotation form has been adopted; the intention would not be to use these for quotation in the text, but to paraphrase for citation purposes. Entries are arranged alphabetically by function; order would differ in text on wind power.

Quotation	Function
Wind is free and, by exploiting it, energy producers accept responsibility for harnessing a natural resource that costs the taxpayer nothing. (Williams, O. 2009. *Free as Air.* Plockton: Highland Press. Page 59.)	Asserting
There is general acknowledgement that, while the cost of oil and gas have risen manyfold over the last three decades, the cost of wind has remained at zero. (*The Energy Journal*, vol. 2, 6–17.)	Comparing
To offer wind power as a feasible alternative to fossil power, the industry would need to provide longitudinal data to demonstrate that the investment could provide a significant return that would make a real difference before investors would back these projects. (Day, A. and Knight, N. 2012. *Investment Economics.* Paris: Gallic Publishing. Page 32.)	Conjecturing
The pro-wind farm lobby has made a concerted pitch to the public that has caused a backlash among the pro-nuclear lobby. (Dow, D. 2011. Agriculture and the Energy Industry. Rome: Dido Press. Page 90.)	Contrasting
Traditional thermal systems of energy production are technically superior in that they are reliable, constant and therefore capable of responding immediately to demand. (Grant, C. 2008. *Fuel Supply and Demand.* Lythe: Glen Publisher. Page 3.)	Describing advantages
Without considerable investment into green energy methods resulting in real alternatives, the UK will experience fuel poverty within the next fifty years. (Logan, J. 2011. *The Power of Energy.* Huddersfield: Holistic Publishers. Page 70.)	Describing cause and effect relations
Wind turbines provide clean energy, for example, no dirty fuel, no waste, no air pollution and no noise. (Hill, T. 2007. *Wind to the Rescue.* Wells: New Press. Page 9.)	Exemplifying
If wind power is tomorrow's fuel, then improved technology in thermal power can ensure that both systems have roles to play in meeting energy needs in the 21st century. (Nott, B. 2010. *Power Merrygoround.* Poole: Ealing Press. Page 41.)	Expressing neutral opinion
If wind power were to be used to supplement the national grid at times of low consumption, then perhaps thermal stations could switch to minimum production. (Unwin, F. 2010. *Power at Source.* Moulton: Minstrel Press. Page 19.)	Conjecturing: disadvantages of wind power

Continued overleaf

Quotation	Function
In Europe, wind farms are now generally sited further offshore than proposed by RWE Npower Renewables Ltd., which currently plans to site Atlantic Array 13km from Lundy Island, 14km from North Devon and 16km from Wales, at its closes points. In Germany all offshore wind farms, and those in the approval process, are at least 35km from shore. (Trust Interim Position Statement, 2011, http://www.nationaltrust.org.uk accessed 12.3.12.)	**Providing data**
Exponents of wind power claim it as a low cost, low maintenance form of power creation, but this misleads since it requires significant amounts of money in terms of land purchase, new infrastructure, capital investment, repair, maintenance and development costs. (Waters, M. 2009. *Powering the Right Way.* Great Portland: Gold Publishing Page 104.)	**Reporting defects in argument**
If wind power were to be used to supplement the national grid at times of low consumption, then thermal stations could switch to minimum production at such times. (Unwin, F. 2010. *Power at Source.* Moulton: Minstrel Press. Page 19.)	**Reporting implications**

PRACTICAL TIPS FOR MANAGING YOUR SOURCE MATERIAL

Return to your brainstorm. We suggested doing an initial brainstorm so that your own ideas were recorded and acted as a basis for researching the literature. As you read more, it is worth going back to your original brainstorm and note which parts of the literature support these 'foundation' ideas so that you can begin to evidence your own ideas from the literature.

Note key contributors to the literature. As you read, you will become aware of names that keep cropping up in the work of others. When you have identified these key thinkers, it would be worth reading some of their work that relates to your own writing. In this way, you will be making your own interpretations of their work and not relying on second-hand analyses done by others. You may, for example, come to different conclusions about the views expressed in these seminal works and may wish to debate them in your writing.

Keep track of web-based material. Increasingly, more use is being made of online materials. Since content can be amended relatively easily, and so can change from day to day, it is important to note the date on which you accessed a web resource as you will need to record this in your references and, perhaps, depending on the citation style you have to use, within the textual citation.

5.1 Analyse the structural models used in your field. In some disciplines, the way that writers go about constructing their texts can be quite formulaic. Look back at Table 5.1 and consider whether the source material in your field favours any particular model over others. This will help you to understand what might be expected of you in your own submissions.

5.2 Evaluate the functions performed within text. Look at an article or book chapter and go through each paragraph identifying what functions (as used in this chapter) that the author has presented in that chapter – for example, describing a situation or process, providing a piece of evidence in support of a particular view, providing evidence refuting a particular view, or reporting the work of another person with which they agree/disagree. Studying how this was done and the language used will again help you to find your 'academic voice' in your writing.

5.3 Analyse the way lecturers use the work of others in their lectures. For many students the whole practice of citation and referencing is new or, at best, different from methods used outside the academic world. Listen carefully to lecturers as they use the literature to support their discussion within a lecture. This will give you an authentic 'live' model which will help you to deepen your understanding of the thinking that underpins the lecture and bring some of the most recent published work to your attention.

PRINCIPLES AND TECHNIQUES FOR REPORTING SOURCE MATERIAL

How to introduce the work of others into your own text

How you choose to present the ideas from the literature in your writing will follow one of two citation options: (i) by direct quotation or (ii) by expressing the idea from the original text using your own words. However, before we can move to the level of detail of quotation and paraphrased citation, it is necessary to take into account, first, the function that you propose to fulfil in your writing by using the cited work (as shown in **Chapter 5**) and, secondly, the selection of an appropriate 'reporting' verb to introduce the information from the source material. This chapter examines how your choice of verb is dictated by the function (purpose) you wish to fulfil in your text.

KEY TOPICS

→ The importance of 'attitude reporting' verbs

→ Citation approaches

→ Use of tense in reporting the work of others

→ Formal style in academic writing

KEY TERMS

Active voice   Attribute   Colloquial   Eponym   Passive voice   Register
Seminal works   Subject   Verb

When you select an idea to include in your work, it is because of its relevance to your discussion. Therefore, to help direct your reader along a particular line of thought and to help build your discussion, your choice of verb reporting the authorship of the source material is important. This verb choice will be dictated by the function you are trying to perform using the source material as supporting evidence. Thus, for example, to demonstrate critical thinking, you may wish to introduce material to:

- provide factual information;
- present evidence that is non-controversial and universally accepted;
- express opinion;
- support or refute ideas or research within your own discussion;
- offer alternative viewpoints or approaches – both positive or negative.

Table 6.1 itemises some reasons that govern the decision to cite the work of others. These factors can be categorised according to whether they mark the beginning of a research theme – the 'received wisdom' in a particular field, or whether they take a positive or a negative view

Table 6.1 Reasons for citing

Received wisdom	Positive	Negative	Process
Indicating key reading to establish the context of work	Validating claims in earlier literature	Critiquing published literature reporting earlier research	Identifying methodology, equipment, etc.
Acknowledging the work of early investigators in a particular field	Acknowledging previous well-received work in a field	Identifying work that is not well-written, or related to existing literature	Authenticating data and classes of fact
Identifying original publications in which an idea or concept was first introduced	Identifying seminal literature	Rejecting the work or ideas of others (negative claims)	Alerting researchers to forthcoming work
Identifying the original publication describing an eponymic concept or terms such as Parkinson's Disease, the Peter Principle, Asperger's Syndrome, or Boyle's Law		Disputing what are sometimes called 'priority claims' of others, that is, questioning claims of 'ownership' of the instigation of a research theme or aspect within it or of ground-breaking achievements	Challenging the validity or merit of the work of others in respect of procedural methods or data interpretation

(Derived from *www.garfield.library.upenn.edu/papers/vladivostok.html*. Accessed 24.3.12.)

of existing literature, or whether they are outlining processes described in the literature. If there is a single 'golden rule', then it is that the citations should be relevant to the purpose of the author making the citations.

THE IMPORTANCE OF 'ATTITUDE REPORTING' VERBS

Whatever your purpose in citing the work of others, in order to make the citation, you will have to attribute the idea to the original author. However, how you report that work will reflect 'attitude' – that could be how the content reflects the work of the original author as perceived in the academic world, or how you view the content. Within your discussion, it makes a considerable difference to interpretation if you report: *Brown contended that* ... (meaning 'disputed in face of controversy') as opposed to: *Brown noted that* ... (meaning 'made special mention of ...') and both take the reader much further in their understanding of the case that has been compiled in the text than simply *Brown said that* ... or *Brown stated that* ... . Table 6.2 provides some examples of positive and negative attitude verbs that are commonly used to report the work of others in academic texts. Thus, your choice of reporting verb reflects your own attitude as well as that of the original author. This helps to construct your own argument and subliminally leads your reader through the analysis you are presenting.

CITATION APPROACHES

Reading the literature helps you to build up a picture of the research within a particular topic area and you will wish to cite some of the sources you have consulted. In several citation styles, two ways of citing are commonly used.

- **Information-prominent citation.** The same names will keep cropping up especially when they have conducted ground-breaking work. Often this work has become part of the accepted background of the study and needs to be acknowledged so that you can evidence your awareness of the development of the field. This kind of work needs to be cited using the information-prominent method.

- **Author-prominent citation.** More recent authors may hold different views or challenge the received wisdom and they should be cited in

Table 6.2 Attitude verbs used to report the work of others. This table derives from analysis of academic discourse across a range of disciplines. This is by no means comprehensive, but it reflects the diversity of expressions used in relation to citing the ideas and work of others.

Attitude verb in past tense	Definition in present tense	Function(s)
Positive connotation examples		
concurred with the view	be in accord	agreeing
supported the view	concur	agreeing
alleged	assert without proof	affirming
asserted	state firmly	affirming/declaring
averred	declare positively	affirming
declared	state emphatically	affirming/alleging
decreed	decide authoritatively	affirming/dictating
professed	claim forcefully	affirming/declaring
contended	dispute in face of controversy	alleging/maintaining
claimed	state to be true when open to question	alleging/maintaining
explained	make understandable	clarifying/simplifying
proclaimed	announce officially and publicly	clarifying
expounded the view	simplify by giving detail	clarifying/elucidating
reflected	make a statement of opinion	commenting/observing
affirmed	maintain to be true	confirming/validating
established	make of truth based on evidence	confirming
conjectured	infer from inconclusive evidence	conjecturing/surmising
guessed	form an opinion with little evidence	conjecturing/surmising
hypothesised	believe tentatively without evidence	conjecturing/theorising
inferred	conclude from evidence or facts	conjecturing/theorising
supposed	consider as a suggestion	conjecturing/suggesting
surmised	infer without sufficient evidence	conjecturing/guessing
defined something as ...	state precise meaning	describing
characterised	categorise	describing
believed	accept as true or real	judging

Continued overleaf

Attitude verb in past tense	Definition in present tense	Function(s)
judged	form an opinion through reasoning	judging/evaluating
commented	explain judgementally	judging/interpreting
held the view	have an opinion	judging/opining
insisted	express an opinion strongly	judging strongly
noted	make special mention of ...	judging/commenting
observed	understand through known facts	judging
opined that ...	express a view	judging/stating belief
posited the view	put forward an idea for consideration	judging/offering opinion
stated	express particulars in words	judging/formulating
suggested	present for consideration	proposing/suggesting
advanced the view	bring to notice	proposing
proposed	put forward for consideration	proposing/proffering
Negative connotation examples		
warned	recommend caution	advising against
diverged	take different routes	differing
disagreed	to have a different opinion	disagreeing with
disputed	question on basis of poor evidence	disagreeing with
doubted	consider unlikely	disagreeing with
opposed	be resistant to an idea	disagreeing with
criticised	judge on basis of good and bad points	disapproving
disdained	regard with scorn	disapproving/despise
questioned the view	express uncertainty	doubting/disputing

a way that requires that the author's name has greater prominence in the text and as part of the sentence rather than in parenthesis at the end of the sentence. This type of work is cited using the author-prominent method.

The two layouts are explained and modelled in the Information box opposite and are modelled within a sample text in Example 6.1.

Differences in citation formats

There are two ways to cite sources in your text. However, guidance as to which should be used, and when, is rarely given routinely to novice writers.

- **Information-prominent citation** is used when the statement being made is regarded as generally accepted in the field of study. For example:

> Providing enough copies of essential texts is a problem for university librarians and this can be a factor in students using the internet as their first research choice (Monaghan, 2012).

Or when the statement relates to literature that is less recent and often provides the foundation of a thread of research or reasoning. For example:

> Books have developed from handwritten texts illuminated by scribes to mass produced paperbacks that bring the printed word to all (Francis, 1991).

Following the Harvard style, as seen in the two examples above, in information-prominent citations the author's name and the date of publication come at the end of the sentence within 'round' brackets which is followed by a full-stop, that is, *after* the final bracket. Generally, no attitude verb is required.

- **Author-prominent citation** is used when the statement is more recent or contemporary. For example:

> O'Donnell (2010) surmised that the implications of downloading lengthy texts from the internet may infringe the intellectual property rights of authors.

As seen in this example, again following the Harvard style, in author-prominent citations the author's name is included as part of the sentence (in this case as the subject of the sentence); date of publication is encased in round brackets and follows the name of the author. Note the consistent use of 'that' immediately or shortly after the verb.

USE OF TENSE IN REPORTING THE WORK OF OTHERS

Citation of the work of others has to be placed in a time-frame. However, there is some inconsistency in practice in that some writers use the present tense to report the literature while others adopt the

Example 6.1 Academic text. This example shows how information-prominent and author-prominent citation is used. In relation to quotation, see **Chapter 7** and to summarising and paraphrasing, see **Chapter 8**.

Plagiarism is not a new phenomenon nor is it one that is confined to academia (Fairfull and Hunter, 1999). In publishing, for example, there are several notorious cases where a best-seller has been shown to be closely similar to another book by another author (Scribner, 2006). However, it is not only with the printed word that plagiarism can occur. Cruikshanks (2002) suggested that plagiarism occurs when an idea originated by a junior member of staff is plagiarised by a senior member who portrays it as their own without any acknowledgement of the true originator of the idea. Peel (1944) asserted that the practice of using someone else's intellectual property without attributing it to the creator of that text, idea or image amounts to theft. Nevertheless, in academia, students have great difficulty with this concept, in part, because they often do not know that plagiarism comes in many different guises – some estimates identify 20 variations (Schneider and Wilkes, 2001). The broad instruction that students should use their own words is often unhelpful because, in many cases, as observed by Ross (2003), they lack the skills of summarising and paraphrasing that would enable them to avoid committing plagiarism. However, Williams (1996) averred that the whole issue of plagiarism raises a more fundamental issue and that is related to critical thinking.

simple past tense. Those who favour the present tense might argue that the text is in front of the reader and therefore it is acceptable to use the present tense (*Brown contends that* ...). However, other writers would argue that:

- the research work has already been done; or
- a view has already been presented for consideration by the academic world.

Hence the simple past tense should be used (*Brown observed that* ...).

The important thing is to ensure that you are consistent in the tense that you use, but note that the present tense is used regardless of time-frame to describe habitual conditions, for example, '*traditionalists argue that* ...'.

FORMAL STYLE IN ACADEMIC WRITING

Traditional academic writing tends towards the formal and you should be aware that the way you write will need to move towards that model (without becoming pompous or complex).

Apocryphal tales emerge from time to time of students who claim that they have been advised that they should have a certain number of citations per page of their writing. This is, of course, nonsensical. A whole string of citations does not add to the merit of writing if these are not germane to the purpose of discussion in the text. It is better to build up a cogent analysis of the existing literature identifying seminal works from which to build the framework of your analysis of the literature. From there you can then include citations that support your particular line of investigation or examine contrasting views or evidence with which you may or may not agree. Sometimes – and increasingly – students use secondary referencing (described more fully in **Chapter 7**). Briefly, this is when a writer cites material that they have not themselves read, but have found in another text that has made use of it. In the context of deciding what to cite, you should always try to find the original source. Historically, secondary references were formerly regarded as unacceptable in some disciplines.

A certain degree of formality can be achieved by being aware of:

- **Register.** Writing for an academic audience should not be complex but you need to be aware of the importance of register, that is, the level of informality or formality that would be expected. For example, it would not be appropriate to write the less formal and more colloquial 'the dictator popped his clogs. LOL'; whereas 'there was much rejoicing when the dictator died' would be acceptable yet simple.

- **Passive voice.** In your reading, you may become aware that the texts do use a more formal style involving the use of the passive. This form of language is used in many disciplines, although it is discouraged in others. The standard electronic grammar checkers

Register in citation writing

Within the style conventions of academic writing, it would not be appropriate to use expressions such as: *Brown said that ...* This language is too informal for academic writing as the register is more reminiscent of oral language which is much more colloquial than that expected in academic writing where *Brown observed that ...* would be acceptable in register. Note that sometimes, people use the expression: *Brown told that ...* This is grammatically incorrect.

will point out when you have used the passive, but you need not take this as an error. It is simply that grammar checkers are generally designed to meet the needs of the business community where the active voice is preferred. If you are unsure about 'active voice' and 'passive voice' look them up in the Glossary at the end of this book.

- **First person singular (I) or plural (we).** Use of the words 'I' and 'we' were taboo in traditional academic writing. However, attitudes have changed, particularly in group work in a research lab or a project group where it is appropriate to acknowledge the work of a team in expressions such as *'We have shown that ...'* which also involve the use of the active voice. In certain disciplines that require writers to report their reflections and feelings, the first person pronoun 'I' is encouraged to show the writer's involvement in the reflection or in reporting observations. As shown in **Chapter 11,** the use of the active voice and first person singular is required in application of the American Psychological Association which frowns emphatically on the use of the passive.

---

i **A technique for using passive voice citations**

In academic writing, views differ about using the passive. Some argue that it sounds overly formal and is difficult to understand while others argue that it helps to maintain objectivity within text. The **passive voice** is used in the example below where author-prominent style citation is used within the sentence structure.

> The view that linguistic skills **have been eroded** and that modern authorship depends on computer expertise is one that **has been criticised** by Sharp (2011).

PRACTICAL TIPS FOR REPORTING FROM SOURCE MATERIAL

Use of tense in reporting the literature. If you are in doubt about which tense to use, then it is probably advisable to stick with the simple past tense (except when reporting habitual conditions). For example:

Brown (1999) **supported** *the view that ...*
Conversely, Smith (2008) **surmised** *that ...*

Be aware of the use of the passive voice in academic writing. A way of being able to identify whether the passive voice has been used in a sentence is to see if it is possible to add 'by x', usually at the end of the sentence. For example:

Early investigations were developed in the lab is the **action**. If the phrase *'by the researchers'* were added, this would identify the **actor** for the reader. Thus: *Early investigations were developed in the lab* (by the researchers).

Look at one of your textbooks and try to find some sentences using the passive voice; decide whether you feel that it contributes to impartiality of the text or whether you feel that it is too wordy.

Ensure that you maintain balance in your analysis of the literature. A frequent weakness in academic writing is that writers often concentrate only on presenting the view they wish to support without analysing alternative views. Exploring alternative viewpoints and giving evidence that argues against these is what adds balance to analyses.

(GO) AND NOW ...

6.1 Expand your 'reporting' vocabulary. Look at some of the texts that you have read in the past which have cited the work of other authors. Check the 'attitude' verbs that have been used to report their work. Add any new verbs to the list given in Table 6.1, making particular note of the function that these performed in the texts.

6.2 Analyse the list of reporting vocabulary. Referring to Table 6.1, identify which verbs might typically be followed by the word 'that'. If you find where 'that' would not follow the verb, then make a particular note of these as a memory aid for your own writing.

6.3 Check through the examples of how to report ideas from the literature. Example 6.1 shows that two citations use the information-prominent citation style and all the others use the author-prominent style using the past tense, with one exception which uses the present tense. Look at the literature in your area and identify whether one of these formats is favoured over another. In the sciences, for example, certain citation styles do not lend themselves to the author-prominent format, preferring to list sources numerically.

QUOTING FROM SOURCE MATERIAL

How to use extracts from other texts correctly

Academic writing is the product of in-depth reading and reflection on your own ideas and the data, conclusions and concepts that you have found in the literature. This material provides you with evidence to support your discussion and which must be cited either by direct quotation or by the use of paraphrasing. The first of these skills as used in academic writing is explored in this chapter; paraphrasing will be addressed in the following chapter.

KEY TOPICS

→ Quotation versus plagiarism

→ Citation information required when quoting

→ Characteristics of quotations

→ Secondary referencing

KEY TERMS

Ampersand   Colon   Direct speech   Ellipsis   Inverted commas
Quotation mark   *sic*   *verbatim*

Quoting text directly from source material has a place in academic writing in many disciplines, whereas, in others, it is rarely used. If used, it is best to be used sparingly since it would be very easy to drift inadvertently into plagiarism (see **Ch 3**).

Before you decide to quote from the literature you have sourced, you should give considerable thought as to why you want to include the exact words used by the original author. Some questions to consider might be:

● does this quotation strengthen my discussion?

● does the extract place special emphasis on the author's findings or viewpoint?

- does the extract present a point that could be counter-argued?
- do the words used make the author's point in a particularly powerful way that would be weakened if paraphrased?

Only if your response to any of these questions is 'yes', should you seriously consider including a quotation.

QUOTATION VERSUS PLAGIARISM

You will need to be discriminating about the number and extent of direct quotations you use in your entire text. Too much quotation can imply plagiarism because, as the text develops, there is a risk that over-quotation can build up unnoticed.

When is quotation plagiarism?

As a 'rule of thumb' in many disciplines, if more than 10 per cent of a piece of work, article, or book chapter is devoted to quotation, this is regarded as a form of plagiarism. The heavy reliance on the literature as a source of words, shows limited original thinking without real analysis or discussion of the issues and may even imply lack of understanding. However, it should be noted that in some disciplines, for example, English literature, more extensive quotation may be expected and thus does not constitute plagiarism.

Shaded text in Example 7.1 shows the amount of quotation in a section of text. Of the total text of 329 words, 200 are copied directly from the source material. This represents 60 per cent of the total word count which would be regarded as unacceptable and probably deemed to be plagiarism. Such dependency on exact wording from the literature would raise serious concerns about the author's limited analysis and lack of broader critical thinking in the new text.

CITATION INFORMATION REQUIRED WHEN QUOTING

To quote correctly, you will need to assemble the following:
- the exact words from the text (sometimes described as '*verbatim* text');

Example 7.1 Over-quotation in text. The shaded text shows the extent of quotation used in the sample.

The whole problem of plagiarism 'raises a more fundamental issue and that is related to critical thinking' (Williams, 1996 cited in Douglas, 2000:67). As Ivor Scott, a well-published academic author frequently cited in academic articles and other texts, declared

> If imitation is the sincerest form of flattery, then finding my words coming back at me *verbatim* in my students' essays should make me exceedingly flattered, but, in fact, makes me incredibly angry. I am not the ultimate authority in my field and I would like to have my words, thoughts and ideas challenged, not copied.   (Scott, 2004:55)

Thus, it is vital that students understand exactly what comprises plagiarism – in all its forms. For academia, 'there is a duty to ensure that students are trained in the skills of citation, referencing, summarising and paraphrasing at an early stage in their studies' (Johns, 1999:25). This will mean that they can use the work of others in a responsible way to support their reasoning and demonstrate 'the skills of critical thinking that distinguish university education' (Chatsworth, 2005:99).

Furthermore, the 'debate on plagiarism has been further confused by the ability of student authors to cut and paste large swathes of text from the internet yet claiming this as their own work' (Watt, 2009:59). Ironically, the ability of academics to track the use of texts of that nature is now similarly facilitated by 'electronic advances that allow for text recognition from databases of hitherto unachievable proportions' (Watson, 2010:19). Graham (2006, cited in Dubhglais, 2009:43) has ventured the opinion that

> The work of the student is compromised by its close affinity with material from other sources and yet, in some instances, the modes of expression in the field are so limited that it is impossible to avoid replicating some structures within a text, even where knowledge of the nature of plagiarism is well-recognised.   (Graham, 2006:43)

The ethical issues involved in detecting and monitoring potential plagiarism are often regarded as being 'not worth the candle'.

- page number(s) or, in the case of journals, volume and page number;
- the publication details. Since different citation styles require different information, you might need all or only some of the following:
  - author(s);
  - date of publication;
  - edition;
  - editor(s);
  - title (of book, chapter or article);
  - journal title (if applicable);
  - place of publication;
  - publisher.

These details in the main should become a routine part of your note-making practice as suggested in **Chapter 4.**

CHARACTERISTICS OF QUOTATIONS

The layout of quotations can differ from one discipline to another, so check the conventions in your particular discipline or subject area. Here are some key guidelines that can help you follow the general rules appropriately.

Quotations should be laid out in one of the following formats:

- **Long quotes** consist of 30 or more words (some propose 40 words) of prose or two or more lines of poetry and should:
  - be indented by five character spaces from the left-hand margin as in Example 7.2;
  - not include quotation marks at the beginning and end; only use quotation marks within the original text where these have been used in the original text;
  - be printed in single line spacing;
  - be followed by the author(s) surname, year of publication and page number separated by a full colon (:) or date of publication followed by page number printed as p. XX, depending on the preferred citation convention.
- **Short quotes** consist of fewer than 30 words and should:
  - be integrated within the sentence as shown in Example 7.3;
  - include the author(s) name within the sentence where it often performs the role of the subject of the sentence. In this case, the date of publication would be in round brackets (...) immediately after the author name; and
  - give the page reference in round brackets (...) at the end of the quotation in the form p. XX.

Both methods are shown in Examples 7.2 and 7.3. Note that punctuation may vary across citation styles, so you should consult your handbook to check for any deviations from the 'official' style.

Quotations should not 'dangle' in the text by appearing without introduction or context so that the reader has no indication of the significance or relevance of the words quoted. Examples 7.2 and 7.3 show how the quotations have been embedded in each sample text.

Example 7.2 Layout for 'long' quotations. The indentation method may be used for 30+ word quotations (or more than three lines of text).

> An essential prerequisite for monitoring demographic trends is efficient garnering of population data which means that the population census is essential to this process. Thus, while early records were relatively primitive in nature, more recent records that have been derived from computerised census data identify the relationship between birth rate and death rate as factors in population growth. This is described as the demographic transition model and is explained by Kay and Campbell (2011) as comprising
>
> > ... four stages: high birth rate with fluctuating but high death rate; high birth rate with falling death rate; falling birth rate and falling death rate; and low birth rate with low death rate. (Kay and Campbell, 2011:23)
>
> More recent studies have attempted to interrogate the demographic transition model in order to identify socio-economic and ethnicity patterns from the birth-rate:death-rate data.

Example 7.3 Layout for 'short' quotations. This style of quotation is used when it is considered that the exact words in the original contribute to the impact of the point being made by the choice of words or language structure. Note that where the quotation forms a part of the sentence, then the full stop is placed *after* the final quotation mark. This is different from the punctuation required in direct speech (the actual words said) in a novel or a newspaper report, for example.

> Simpson (1953) claimed that one factor affecting the demographic transition model involved 'the changing roles of women as key contributors to the economy since these roles impact on their traditional child-bearing roles' (p. 63).

SECONDARY REFERENCING

Secondary referencing occurs when a writer cites a source that they have not read themselves. This could be because the original is out of print or unavailable to them for other reasons. In this case the item that is cited is the text that they read personally. Traditionally, secondary referencing, sometimes called secondary citation, was actively discouraged or even disallowed. However, with the ease of access to online literature, the incidence of secondary quotation is more common. Example 7.4 uses Harvard style to cite a secondary reference in the text. Note that the source listed in the references is the text that the writer read, not the reference for the unread text.

When should I use single and double quotation marks? ?

There are two systems that apply here relating to quotation marks, sometimes called 'inverted commas': one follows British English and the other American English conventions.

British English: Single quotation marks are used around the text to mark the exact words spoken or written. Any quote-within-the-quote is placed in double quotation marks.

American English: Double quotation marks are used around the text to mark the exact words spoken or written. Any quote-within-the-quote is placed in single quotation marks.

Note that these conventions apply in most cases but there are some disciplines which do not follow them. Consult your handbook or academic advisor if the required style differs from these.

What's the difference between 'curly' quotes and 'straight' quotes? ?

'Curly' or 'round' quotes are the inverted comma symbols that were found traditionally on typewriters. Sometimes in word processing packages these are referred to as 'smart quotes'. The single ones look like this: ' and ' double ones look like " or ". They resemble miniature digits 6 or 66 before the quotation words and digits 9 or 99 after the quotation. Note that the ' and " coming after the quotation come immediately after the last letter or the full stop, that is without a character space, otherwise they will 'read' the space as the beginning of a new sentence and revert to the digit 6 in shape.

'Straight' quotes are the inverted comma symbols that are often used by word processors as a single downward stroke. The single ones look like this: ' and double ones look like this: ''. There is no difference in form between the straight quotes before and after the quotation.

'Curly' and 'straight' styles of quotation marks should not be mixed within the same document. Indeed, where this happens, it can be a tell-tale sign of plagiarism where text including punctuation has been cut and pasted into a piece of writing.

Permitted 'alteration' to the text of a quotation: ellipsis, square brackets and use of *sic*

Ellipsis …: Sometimes only part of the text is relevant to your purpose and you can quite legitimately omit the irrelevant section by inserting three dots (ellipsis) to replace the omitted text providing that the sentence flow is maintained. An example of ellipsis is shown in the quotation below.

> Twitter-feed and other social network interactions have been harnessed by academics as they attempt to stimulate more engagement with course content … and improve discussion on debate-worthy issues that seems to be increasingly lacking in tutorials.

Square brackets [...]: In some instances a quotation does not make sense within the flow of the sentence you want to create. In this case you can insert a word or words inside square brackets to make the sense that you need to make the sentence read correctly. In the example below the words 'the e-book' have been inserted by the writer to explain what is meant by 'it'.

> Gunn (2008) observed that while 'it [the e-book] might be regarded as an alternative to the textbook, both have a place in enhancing learning'.

***sic*:** This is a Latin word meaning 'thus' in the sense of 'in the same way'. It is used to indicate that a writer recognises an error in the original quotation ('loss' in the example below) but has chosen to retain the error to remain faithful to the original source. The insertion of the word '*sic*' after the error implies '*it was in this way in the original*'. This can be seen in the following quotation where the word before '*sic*' should be 'lost'. Note that the word 'sic' is italicised because it is a non-English word.

> Smyth (2012) claimed that 'students have loss [*sic*] their ability to read and understand long pieces of text'.

Conventions about citing multiple authors in academic text

***et al.*:** Academics often collaborate in their research and in their writing, which can present a writer who wishes to cite the work of multiple authors with potential difficulties. For example, where the list of authors is a lengthy one – especially in the scientific community – including all the authors in the citation in the text would be cumbersome and interrupt the flow of the text too much. Consequently, use has been made of the Latin expression '*et al.*' which is short for '*et alii*' meaning 'and other people/and others'. In modern usage, this form is adopted since it represents mixed gender groups and thus is more inclusive. Since '*al*' is abbreviated, it is followed by a full-stop. Thus, '*et al.*' is used within the text when referring to three or more authors. Hence:

> Lyon *et al.* (2010) suggested that 'total hip replacement could only be as good as the materials used for the prosthetics'.

Some academics prefer to abandon the Latin and simply use the English words 'and others' which would appear as:

> Ludd and others (2010) suggested that 'any system using the alternative transferable vote (ATV) must be riddled with problems notably voters' difficulties in understanding how it works'.

Note that in most referencing systems, '*et al.*' would not be used in the reference list; instead, all authors would be named.

Note also that in a scientific citation where multiple authors have contributed to a text, then the convention X *et al.* is used if X is the principal investigator (PI) and is the first named author, however, X and co-workers is used where X is the principal investigator but the journal uses a system of naming contributors in alphabetical order.

Styles using naming and numbering systems are explained in Part 2.

Ampersand (&): This symbol is an abbreviation deriving from the Latin word for 'and'. It is used in some citation and referencing systems where there are two authors, for example:

> Tang & Lee (2011) averred that 'computer-aided design (CAD) would bring modern architectural design within the grasp of people of modest means'.

For other purposes, the ampersand, being an abbreviation, is regarded as too informal for academic contexts and should not be used. Instead the word 'and' should be used.

Example 7.4 Two examples of secondary referencing. These examples use the form of words 'cited in' but it would be equally acceptable to use the form 'quoted in' where material had been quoted. Secondary referencing can be used in paraphrased citations as well as in direct quotations.

An **information-prominent secondary citation** would be presented as:

> One of the most powerful criticisms is that reading on-screen is, for many people, a painful activity (Owen, 2007 cited in Peel, 2009).

An **author-prominent secondary citation** would be presented as:

> Owen (2007 cited in Peel, 2009) considered that 'one of the most powerful criticisms of reading on-screen is that, for many people, this is a painful activity'.

 PRACTICAL TIPS FOR QUOTING AS A CITATION METHOD

Keep a running total of the words that make up the quotes in your work. This may seem to be a tedious chore but it will ensure that you do not over-run the 10 per cent rule about *verbatim* content in your work. This could save you a lot of time later if you do not have to 'unpick' a number of quotations and then rework your text to accommodate the ideas in your own words.

Avoid secondary referencing if at all possible. Wherever possible, you should try to trace and read the original literature by the primary author rather than rely on secondary referencing. There are at least two good reasons for this: the first is that you run the risk of appearing lazy in riding on the back of someone else's work and the second is that you have to rely on the accuracy and impeachable intent of the secondary author's interpretation of the primary author's work. You may find that your trust has been misplaced, hence it is wise to go back to the primary source if you can.

Discriminate between British and American English. You may be consulting sources that are published in the USA and so you should be conscious of different rules regarding some aspects of punctuation as well as spelling rules that differ from those in the UK. If you are quoting from an American source, then you need to remain faithful to the American spelling in the original rather than using British English spelling conventions. You should also be aware that, in some software packages, the default is for American English which can appear on the screen even when you selected British English.

Use ellipsis carefully. When you decide to shorten the quotation you have decided to use, ensure that the removal of some of the words from the original which are then replaced by ellipsis (...) does not change the meaning of the quotation. If the word 'not' were to be removed in the previous sentence, then it would clearly change the meaning entirely.

Look for 'dangling' quotations in textbooks and your own text. This practice probably stems from a common strategy for creative writing in school where a quotation was used as an introduction and to inspire the writer. Sometimes, this technique spills over into university writing where it can be introduced at the beginning or randomly in the text. The quotation is included for its broad relevance to the topic but it is not discussed or related to the content of the full text – hence 'dangling'. It is advisable to avoid using this 'dangling' quotation as it will make your work seem incomplete and possibly incoherent.

(GO) AND NOW ...

7.1 Check the conventions for presentation of quotes in your own discipline. You may find specific information about quotation in your course handbook or the guidelines for dissertations and theses or instructions to authors. If this is not covered, then you should ask your lecturer, supervisor or journal editor for their preference before you submit your final version. This will save you considerable time and is preferable to having to revise an entire text in order to meet the requirements at the last minute.

7.2 Confirm the acceptability of secondary referencing in your discipline. Some academics are particularly rigid on this point and will not permit secondary referencing in texts in any circumstance, while others are more relaxed on this. However, although the trend towards secondary referencing seems to be driven by the accessibility to diverse resources via the internet, there is often difficulty in accessing more obscure sources and journal articles. If your university library does not have a subscription to these, you may only be able to get as far as accessing the abstract rather than the full journal. You may need to verify the position in your area by asking a member of academic staff.

7.3 Get to know punctuation terms. If you are unfamiliar with any of the terms relating to punctuation used in this chapter or you would like to review what these are, then you may find it useful to look at 'Rules of punctuation' in Appendix 3.

SUMMARISING AND PARAPHRASING

How to use your own words to express the work of others

As noted in **Chapter 7**, quotation must be used sparingly and so the alternative strategies of summarising and paraphrasing are more frequently used. Thus, you will need to develop these strategies for your own writing by learning how to deconstruct the meaning of text and find other ways of expressing the content without heavy reliance on the wording and structure of the original.

KEY TOPICS

→ Distinctions between summarising and paraphrasing

→ Using summarising and paraphrasing in your own work

→ A strategy for summarising

→ Strategies for paraphrasing

KEY TERMS

Gravitas Paraphrase Summarise Syntax Topic paragraph
Topic sentence

While quotation replicates an author's words, the central concept of both summarising and paraphrasing is that writers use their own words rather than those of the original author, except:

● where, within the paraphrase or summary, a direct quotation from the source document is used; or

● where there is use of same or similar wording to state aspects that are common knowledge, for example, dates, well-known facts or anything regarded as published in the public domain in information/reference sources such as dictionaries or encyclopaedias; or

● where 'shared', subject-specific terms have been used in the original.

DISTINCTIONS BETWEEN SUMMARISING AND PARAPHRASING

In both summarising and paraphrasing the final text will normally be shorter than the original text. The point is to distil the essence of meaning from the original but with important differences.

- **Summarising:** while recognising that technical terms or 'shared language' can be retained, use your own words in writing to:
  - give the general idea;
  - state the main points briefly;
  - include only the views of the original author
  ... but giving less detail than in a paraphrase.
- **Paraphrasing:** while recognising that technical terms or 'shared language' can be retained, use your own words in writing to:
  - explain the key idea(s);
  - clarify their meaning;
  - include only the views of the original author
  ... but giving more detail than in a summary.

The differences between these two approaches to restating the work of others are modelled in Example 8.1. As well as indicating variation in content, the examples demonstrate visually the relative difference in length. Paraphrasing will reduce the original text but not as much as a summary which will be significantly shorter than the original text.

USING SUMMARISING AND PARAPHRASING IN YOUR OWN WORK

When you decide to include the work of another in your text, you need to treat each citation as unique. As explained in **Chapter 4**, you will have evaluated the text and so have a reason for choosing to incorporate material from the literature. This will reflect the function that citation will perform within your text – supporting your viewpoint, critiquing other views and so on (see Table 4.3). This may also dictate whether you wish to introduce an idea in more general terms by summarising or elucidate a discussion in greater detail by paraphrasing.

Example 8.1 Summarised and paraphrased text. The two sample texts show the differences in wordage as well as content in summarised and paraphrased versions. (Both examples follow the Harvard Style.)

Original text consists of 51 words.

E-books are a function of the internet era and make access to otherwise unattainable material possible to wider audiences. The globalisation of literature means that individual authors can present their work to a wider audience without incurring abortive publication costs. This facility constitutes a considerable threat to publishers of traditional books. [*51 words*]

Source: Watt, W. (2006) *The demise of the book.* Cambridge: The Printing Press (page 13)

A. Summarised text follows information-prominent style

With the advent of e-books, individual authors are faced with new approaches to publication of their work (Watt, 2006).

B. Paraphrased text follows author-prominent citation (Table 6.4)

Watt (2006) notes that there is concern amongst publishers of hard-copy printed books that the advent of e-books marks the end of their monopoly of the literature market since authors can publish directly from the internet thus avoiding publishing costs.

Checking on terms ✔

Vocabulary expands through the experience of assimilating new words. When studying in a specialist academic area, you may find that the literature frequently presents you with new or unfamiliar words. Check these out in a dictionary or thesaurus so that you absorb these new words and even note them down if they have a special meaning within your own field. This will also help you remember the spelling.

A STRATEGY FOR SUMMARISING

Stage 1: Identify the main idea or theme:

● Read the topic and terminator paragraphs to identify the main ideas of the text.

● Read the topic sentences of the intervening paragraphs allocating a defining term to each paragraph to identify the main topic, point, argument or counter-argument presented within it. Write these terms as a list of words; to give you an overview of the whole text.

i Bad summarising and paraphrasing: a *caveat*

As noted in Chapter 1, one form of plagiarism occurs when words similar in meaning (synonyms) are used as replacements for some words in the text; another form of plagiarism occurs when sentences are simply re-ordered or restructured using the same wording as the original text. Unfortunately, as an internet search shows, school-age learners and those for whom English is not a first language are encouraged to substitute synonyms and re-order sentence content and sequence in writing summaries or paraphrasing. To what end is unclear because these activities only really demonstrate 'word juggling' skills rather than demonstration of deeper understanding of the concepts expressed in the original text. This explains, in part, why there is confusion about word substitution and sentence switching being improper in the context of serious, university level academic writing. This chapter outlines some strategies which help avoid these bad habits.

- Highlight points of particular relevance to your reason for citing this source material.
- Go back and read the whole text (or the section most relevant to your own purpose).

Stage 2: Leave the text and do something else for a spell, then:

- Return to the task and *without looking at your notes* and using your own words, try to write down your recollection of the main theme(s) and complementary points.
- Check your version with your earlier notes; add in anything that you have omitted.

Stage 3: Using your 'own word' version, remove unnecessary words or change word order or syntax to create shorter sentences or phrases.

Stage 4: Starting by signposting the author, identify the main theme and key points, explaining how the main theme will form part of the discussion in your own text. Although the example in Example 8.2 models the summary as a single sentence, a summary can extend to a number of sentences. Note that it is equally acceptable to use the information-prominent format to present a summary (Example 7.4).

Example 8.2 Model of summarising stages. The original text is reduced over the four stages from 125 words to 17 words. The strategy modelled is a useful one when trying to reduce the word count on your own text, often when you have laboured a point and need to make it more succinctly.

Original text with source ➡	Stage 1: ➡ Topic per sentence	Stage 2: ➡ Essential content as expanded own word text	Stage 3: Further reductions finishing with final version
The learning that students experience within their school education primes them for exam-taking and not for higher education.	Exams in school	School education driven by exam criteria	School driven by exam criteria
For many subjects taught at further education levels, the emphasis is similarly placed on attaining module passes achieved after several iterations of assignments have been submitted, amended and resubmitted.	Colleges repeated iterations	Further education multiple drafts to achieve module passes	Further education multiple drafts for module passes
The overall effect is to provide students new to higher education with several perceptions that do not necessarily pertain in universities.	Students' mistaken views	Mistaken view that university wants 'right answers' and repetition of ideas presented by staff	University wants 'right answers' and repetition of staff ideas.
These include, for example, the beliefs that there are 'always "right" answers and that what will be rewarded is the information provided by lecturers.'	Always 'right' answer		Critical thinking skills wanted at university
The ability to exercise "critical thinking" skills is an expectation of academia	Critical thinking expected	Critical thinking skills wanted at university	Students fail if unaware of study 'rules' at university [37 words]
and it is when students fail to recognise this concept as the new rules of the game that they are most likely to fail.	Student failure and new rules of game [21 words]	Students fail if unaware of study 'rules' at university [48 words]	School exam criteria
McMillan, K. 2009. *Elaborating expectation in higher education.* Dundee, Tay Press. [125 words]			Further education multiple drafts for passes
			University wants 'right answers' and repetition of staff ideas.
			Critical thinking skills at university
			Students lack 'rules' at university [30 words]
			Stage 4: Final summary
			McMillan (2009) claims that schools and colleges have misled students' understanding of University 'rules' on critical thinking. [17 words]

STRATEGIES FOR PARAPHRASING

Different methods are suggested to achieve a good paraphrase of a text. Three approaches are modelled in Example 8.3:

1 **Underlining approach** – reduces content in three different stages to achieve the paraphrase.

2 **Reporters' questions** – this is less onerous and will not suit all source text types but it allows deconstruction of the original text and gives a strategy for engaging with the original meaning and intention of the text.

3 **Theme re-grouping approach** – this is probably the most challenging of the three approaches but the one that distances the secondary writer furthest from the original and thus the least likely to involve unintentional plagiarism.

One method may suit your learning and writing style more than the others.

Example 8.3 (a) **Paraphrasing – Method 1: underlining approach**

Original text: **Academic text reporting interview findings**

However, there is a further twist. The students interviewed acknowledged unanimously the need for greater learner autonomy in higher education as opposed to school, but they frequently resorted to seeking the advice or opinions of others, mostly teaching staff. This may relate to the school-induced preoccupation with finding the 'right answer' and that may explain lack of confidence in exercising critical skills supported by evidence. It may also account for the heavy reliance on the language used in text as being acceptable within the genres in which they are required to write.

Another primary anxiety that emerged concerned the potential for peer ridicule although, in practice, there were no formal university situations in which they would be exposed to this kind of criticism. It seemed that this anxiety stemmed from school experiences where, by some kind of reverse logic, it was seen as socially unacceptable to make errors but conversely unacceptable to 'show off' by knowing the right answers. University thus came as something of a riddle to such students who reported that they found it difficult to know how to go about the 'right answers' that they felt were expected.

This need to seek affirmation could be explained as a developmental issue for all students, regardless of level or background, as they adjust to the more sophisticated thought processes of higher education. Among first year students the fear of 'getting it wrong' was acknowledged. They perceived that not knowing the 'right answer' left them particularly weakened in examinations where there was no opportunity to consult with others and

---

where what they wrote was entirely their own. It follows, therefore, that what they produced in an examination was possibly a more accurate demonstration of their own understanding than work done alongside others.

These concerns led many students to write 'model answers' which they cross-referenced with their lecture notes and then memorised. The assumption was that what they heard in lectures would be what the lecturers wanted to read in exam answers was not only misplaced as a strategy, but was made nonsensical by the fact that the people grading exam scripts came from across the department and would not necessarily have specific knowledge of lecture content.

By contrast, other students reported that they resorted to writing down all that they knew on a topic regardless of relevance. Interestingly, others admitted that they write down what they can express in written form and this is not necessarily the totality of their knowledge or understanding on a topic. Thus, establishing the real level of a student's understanding of academic topics from their writing is difficult to gauge. [*434 words*]

Source: McMillan, K. (2012) *Evaluating student understanding.* Dundee, Tay Press.

Stage 1: **Using selective underlining**

However, there is <u>a further twist</u>. The students interviewed acknowledged <u>unanimously</u> the need for <u>greater learner autonomy</u> in <u>higher education</u> as opposed <u>to school</u>, but they frequently resorted to <u>seeking the advice or opinions</u> of others, mostly <u>teaching staff</u>. This may relate to the <u>school-induced</u> preoccupation with finding the <u>'right answer'</u> and that may explain <u>lack of confidence</u> in exercising <u>critical skills</u> supported by evidence. It may also account for the <u>heavy reliance on the language used in text</u> as being <u>acceptable</u> within the genres in which they are required to write.

Another primary anxiety that emerged concerned the potential for <u>peer ridicule</u> although, in practice, there were <u>no formal university situations</u> in which they would be exposed to this kind of criticism. It seemed that this anxiety stemmed from <u>school experiences</u> where, by some kind of reverse logic, it was seen as <u>socially unacceptable to make errors</u> but conversely <u>unacceptable to 'show off' by knowing the right answers</u>. <u>University</u> thus came as something of a riddle to such students who reported that they found it <u>difficult</u> to know how to <u>go about the 'right answers'</u> that they felt were expected.

This need to seek affirmation could be explained as a <u>developmental issue</u> for all students, regardless of level or background, as they <u>adjust</u> to the more sophisticated <u>thought processes of higher education</u>. Among first year students the <u>fear of 'getting it wrong'</u> was acknowledged. They perceived that not knowing the 'right answer' left them particularly <u>weakened in examinations</u> where there was <u>no opportunity to consult</u> with others and where what they <u>wrote was entirely their own.</u> It follows, therefore, that what they <u>produced in an examination</u> was possibly a more accurate demonstration of <u>their own understanding</u> than work done alongside others.

These concerns led many students <u>to write 'model answers'</u> which they <u>cross-referenced</u> with their <u>lecture notes</u> and then <u>memorised</u>. The assumption was that what they heard

Continued overleaf

in <u>lectures</u> would be what the <u>lecturers wanted</u> to read in <u>exam answers</u> was not only <u>misplaced</u> as a strategy but was made nonsensical by the fact that the <u>people grading</u> exam scripts came from <u>across the department</u> and would <u>not</u> necessarily have <u>specific knowledge of lecture content</u>.

By contrast, <u>other students</u> reported that they resorted to <u>writing down all that they knew</u> on a topic <u>regardless of relevance</u>. Interestingly, others admitted that they <u>write down what they can express</u> in written form and this is <u>not</u> necessarily the <u>totality of their knowledge</u> or understanding on a topic. <u>Thus, establishing the real level of a student's understanding of academic topics from their writing is difficult to gauge.</u>

Stage 2: Eliminating extra words

<u>a further twist</u>   <u>unanimously</u>   <u>greater learner autonomy</u>
<u>higher education</u>   <u>to school</u>   <u>seeking the advice or opinions</u>
<u>teaching staff.</u>   <u>school-induced</u>   <u>'right answer'</u>   <u>lack of confidence</u>
<u>critical skills</u>   <u>heavy reliance on the language used in text</u>   <u>acceptable peer ridicule</u>
<u>no formal university situations</u>   <u>school experiences</u>   <u>socially unacceptable to make errors</u>
<u>unacceptable to 'show off' by knowing the right answers.</u>   <u>University</u>   <u>difficult</u>
<u>go about the 'right answers'</u>   <u>developmental issue</u>   <u>adjust</u>
<u>thought processes of higher education.</u>   <u>fear of 'getting it wrong'</u>
<u>weakened in examinations</u>   <u>no opportunity to consult</u>   <u>wrote was entirely their own.</u>
<u>produced in an examination</u>   <u>their own understanding</u>   <u>to write 'model answers'</u>
<u>cross-referenced lecture notes</u>   <u>memorised.</u>   <u>lectures</u>
<u>lecturers wanted in exam answers</u>   <u>misplaced</u>   <u>people grading</u>
<u>across the department</u>   <u>not specific knowledge of lecture content.</u>
<u>other students writing down all that they knew</u>   <u>regardless of relevance,</u>
<u>write down what they can express</u>   <u>not totality of their knowledge</u>
<u>Thus, establishing the real level of a student's understanding of academic topics from their writing is difficult to gauge.</u> [*162 words*]

Stage 3: Rewording ideas

McMillan (2012) suggested that there is an inherent difficulty in establishing true levels of students' understanding through examination of their writing. Drawing from two examples, she identified that students had perceptions about levels of correctness in their answers which inhibited their writing but also caused concern about looking stupid. She attributes these attitudes to behaviours in schools. Although greater autonomy at university was recognised by the subjects in the study, their actions contradicted this. Four particular strategies were identified: memorising pre-constructed text; reflecting lecture content in their writing; seeking the correct answers from staff; writing down all they know indiscriminately; or writing within the limitations of their ability to express themselves in writing. [*113 words*]

Comment: This writer referring to McMillan (2012) could have used that source to support discussion on, for example:

- Difficulty in assessing depth of knowledge.
- Strategies students adopt as survival strategies.
- Differences between writing at school and at university.

Not all these ideas from the original have been included in the paraphrase above. This demonstrates that the new text only need include the points relating to the purpose that the writer has in citing the text – giving examples, arguing, describing, stressing points or justifying a viewpoint.

Note word length differences between paraphrase and original text.

Example 8.3(b) Paraphrasing – Method 2: using the reporters' questions

Who? Author: K. McMillan **What?** Student writing and right/wrong answers **When?** 2012 **Where?** School versus university **Why?** Assess levels of knowledge from writing **How?** Student interviews	McMillan (2012) **[Who 1]** conducted student **[Who 2]** interviews **[How 1]** to examine ways in which student writing demonstrated abilities in critical thinking reflecting their knowledge and understanding **[Why]**. The interview responses **[How 2]** suggested that students in university acknowledge the need for greater independence of thought at university when compared with school **[Where 1]** but nevertheless relied on strategies that helped them to produce what they perceived would be right answers **[What 1]**. These strategies in exams included writing all that they knew about a topic **[What 2]**; memorising set-piece answers modelled on their lectures **[What 3]**; or using exact words from resource material **[What 4]**. Since they were fearful of giving incorrect answers and of peer ridicule **[What 5]** such as they had experienced at school **[Where 2]**, they spent time seeking confirmation of right answers from their teachers **[What 1 + How 3]**. The conclusion reached was that these behaviours made it difficult to estimate the extent of students' understanding through their writing. [*138 words*]

Comment: This method may be more helpful in practical subjects but its essence is applicable to a number of situations. The technique requires:

● Reading of original.

● Selective underlining as in Method 1 above.

● Turning over original.

● Answering reporters' questions for framework without reference to the text.

● Writing to each point and restructuring order to perform function (purpose) required for the new writer's text.

Note word length differences between paraphrase and original text.

Example 8.3(c) Paraphrasing – Method 3: theme re-grouping approach

Key points	Original text
Paragraph 1 **1.1** Debate distortion **1.2** Seeking confirmation **1.3** Conjecturing re critical skills **1.4** Using original wording	However, there is a further twist. The students interviewed acknowledged unanimously the need for greater learner autonomy in higher education as opposed to school [**1.1**], but they frequently resorted to seeking the advice or opinions of others, mostly teaching staff. [**1.2**] This may relate to the school-induced preoccupation with finding the 'right answer' and that may explain lack of confidence in exercising critical skills [**1.3**] supported by evidence. It may also account for the heavy reliance on the language used in text [**1.4**] as being acceptable within the genres in which they are required to write.
Paragraph 2 **2.1** Potential peer scorn **2.2** School anxiety **2.3** Negative perceptions **2.4** Difficulties finding right answers	Another primary anxiety that emerged concerned the potential for peer ridicule although, in practice, there were no formal situations in which they would be exposed to this kind of criticism [**2.1**]. It seemed that this anxiety stemmed from school experiences where [**2.2**], by some kind of reverse logic, it was seen as socially unacceptable to make errors but conversely unacceptable to 'show off' by knowing the right answers [**2.3**]. University thus came as something of a riddle to such students who reported that they found it difficult to know how to go about the 'right answers' [**2.4**] that they felt were expected.
Paragraph 3 **3.1** Student development **3.2** Anxiety over mistakes **3.3** Implications in exams **3.4** Exams as real knowledge	This need to seek affirmation could be explained as a developmental issue for all students, regardless of level or background [**3.1**], as they adjust to the more sophisticated thought processes of higher education. Among first year students the fear of 'getting it wrong' [**3.2**] was acknowledged. They perceived that not knowing the 'right answer' left them particularly weakened in examinations [**3.3**] where there was no opportunity to consult with others and where what they wrote was entirely their own. It follows, therefore, that what they produced in an examination was possibly a more accurate demonstration of their own understanding [**3.4**] than work done alongside others.
Paragraph 4 **4.1** Memorising model answers **4.2** Misplaced use of lectures	These concerns led many students to write 'model answers' [**4.1**] which they cross-referenced with their lecture notes [**4.2**] and then memorised. [**4.1**] The assumption was that what they heard in lectures would be what the lecturers wanted to read in exam answers was not only misplaced [**4.2**] as a strategy but was made nonsensical by the fact that the people grading exam scripts came from across the department and would not necessarily have specific knowledge of lecture content.

Key points	Original text
Paragraph 5 **5.1** Writing everything **5.2** Writing within ability to express **5.3** Conclusion	By contrast, other students reported that they resorted to writing down all that they knew [5.1] on a topic regardless of relevance. Interestingly, others admitted that they write down what they can express in written form [5.2] and this is not necessarily the totality of their knowledge or understanding on a topic. Thus, establishing the real level of a student's understanding of academic topics from their writing is difficult to gauge [5.3].

Paraphrase against numbered key points

McMillan (2012) suggested that students adopt strategies at university which indicate that they are still heavily influenced by their school experiences [**2.2**] in relation to the correctness of their answers [**1.3**]. Their anxieties relating to peer ridicule should they make errors by giving 'wrong answers' continue to be strong although there is little likelihood that they will experience this at university [**2.1**]. They go to considerable lengths to ensure they have the 'right answers' particularly in exams [**3.3**] where they write down all that they have the ability to express [**5.2**] or randomly write all they know [**5.1**]. Some resort to using exact words from texts while [**1.4**]others memorise set piece answers [**4.1**] based on lectures although feeding back lecture content is not appropriate in higher education [**4.2**]. These attitudes and strategies appear to indicate weak critical thinking skills [**4.3**] but for the reasons described the extent of students' understanding is difficult to estimate on the basis of their writing [**5.3**]. [*155 words*]

Comment: This paraphrase has been achieved by identifying the key point or function in the original. For the purposes of modelling this technique, numbers have been allocated to each point but this would not be necessary in practice. The paraphrasing technique takes a point midway in the original, in this case, point 2.2, and works over the text such that it develops the ideas in a way that shifts the emphasis to the one that the writer citing this work wishes to stress in their own discussion.

Note that although there is some shared language in the paraphrase, this is acceptable.

Again, not all ideas have been included from the original.

Compare word length differences between paraphrase and original text.

The advantage of summarising and paraphrasing in these ways is that there is much less risk of plagiarism because you are using your own words and writing style to create the shorter version; you are also demonstrating your ability to engage with the material and reach conclusions that demonstrate your critical thinking skills. In addition, as you become more practised and at ease with the process, you will be able to summarise or paraphrase by omitting some of the stages. In addition, these approaches will help you to achieve a deeper understanding of the text and allow you to exploit the ideas more effectively in your own analysis.

? Can I cite lectures in my work?

The aim of lectures is to guide students to think through a topic by supplementing their own reflection with further reading. In some cultures, citing the lecturer/lectures is done as a mark of respect, but in UK universities lecturers would generally not wish to have their own work fed back to them. This is because lectures are intended to explore key issues, perhaps by presenting alternative views or approaches to a topic, giving direction on further reading or investigation. Lectures are not intended to be simply for dissemination of facts or other forms of information; they are a guide for further work by the individual. Thus, citing the lecturer is perceived as demonstrating lack of initiative, lack of understanding, lack of critical thinking skills, in short, lack of good academic practice.

PRACTICAL TIPS FOR SUMMARISING AND PARAPHRASING

Keep it simple. When you summarise or paraphrase, omit any examples or detailed figures as these will obscure the key ideas that you are wanting to explain. If your readers want more detail then they can go to the source document. Paraphrase only what you need to support your own writing rather than encompass the complete original; this is definitely a case of less is more.

Observe copyright. Copyright law 'allows you to protect your original material and stop others from using your work without permission' (Intellectual Property Office 2009, www.ipo.gov.uk/c-benefit.htm).

Since, in the UK, authors have literary copyright for a further 70 years and publishers have typographical copyright for 25 years, it is important that you acknowledge the source of ideas that you wish to include in your writing.

Be objective. Avoid value judgements (see Glossary) and distance yourself from becoming emotionally entangled in the debate no matter how strong your own feelings on a topic; your writing will gain more *gravitas* if you offer reasoned argument and recognised evidence in support of your position.

Avoid synonyms and sentence juggling. Whatever you may have been told at earlier points in your education about paraphrasing using strategies of changing single words or re-ordering the sentences as they appeared in the original text, ignore this for academic writing for university level. It is regarded as plagiarism (see **Ch 3**). Experiment with the strategies offered in this chapter so that you become more skilled and confident about expressing ideas in your own words and style.

Revisit some of the literature to identify balance in use of quotation, summarising and paraphrasing. Each of the citation strategies will be used in some academic texts but not in others. Use a sample of the literature in your area to analyse the places where the author has used quotation, summarised source material and paraphrased. This will give you further insights into the discourse styles and conventions within your own subject area. This should also give you some ideas about using these techniques in your own writing.

GO AND NOW ...

8.1 Look at the case study in Chapter 9. This case study has been provided to show you the complete process covered in Part 1 and is based on a particular topic so that you can see how the total sequence develops up to the final draft. It is presented using the Harvard style to illustrate citation within an authentic text. The style of citation that you are expected to use might be different.

8.2 Move on to compare different referencing methods. Look at **Five Referencing Styles** which presents some of the more common referencing methods. It is very likely that the style of citation and referencing that you are expected to follow will be prescribed by your supervisor, department or discipline. However, since you may well have to read from sources that do not follow this style, it is important to familiarise yourself with some of the features of other styles, for example, number systems as opposed to name–date systems.

8.3 Look at the Appendix for additional tips on precision in writing. The Appendix contains sections on punctuation as this relates to citation and referencing, spelling and grammar points that often cause some difficulties in academic writing, especially where the citation and referencing style require the adoption of particular approaches to writing the text. You may need to review your understanding of some aspects of grammar in order to conform to these requirements.

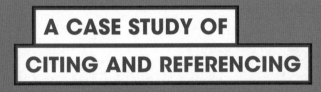

**A CASE STUDY OF
CITING AND REFERENCING**

9

A SAMPLE TEXT TO DEMONSTRATE CITATION CONVENTIONS IN PRACTICE

How to complete the process from initial brainstorm to final text

As you become more experienced in the conventions and aspects of attribution in academic writing, you will find that you can write effectively and quickly when analysing the literature. Earlier chapters have described individual stages in the journey from first brainstorm through to citation. Here, in a model text, we demonstrate how this process comes together.

KEY TOPICS

→ Scenario

→ Brainstorming the topic

→ Identifying the literature

→ Isolating the literature content

→ Organising by function

→ Evolving the language structures

→ Integrating citations into the work

→ Compiling the reference list

KEY TERM

Authorities

This chapter exemplifies the processes of citation, referencing and plagiarism avoidance through an example of academic writing, as it might be carried out by a typical student.

Andrew has been asked to write a paper in which he is required to evaluate the merits of e-books as a relatively recent development of e-technology. The task is open-ended in that he has not been given a particular direction in which to take his appraisal of the topic.

BRAINSTORMING THE TOPIC

Andrew has constructed a brainstorm of his own ideas before he looks at the available literature. This is shown in Figure 9.1 and has allowed Andrew to shape his thoughts into themes which might help him to analyse the topic methodically.

IDENTIFYING THE LITERATURE

Andrew knows that there are other viewpoints that have been discussed in the literature. His research has provided him with source material that looks at some of the issues. He is aware that this is a relatively new area and that little may be published on it. Hence, he may have to look at some online material which may be the most up-to-date available, although its rigour as source material for academic purposes may be suspect. Therefore, he may ask for some help from the subject librarian to find more reputable resources. Example 9.1 lists the 15 resources that Andrew, with the help of his librarian, has managed to track down.

ISOLATING THE LITERATURE CONTENT

From the resources he has found, Andrew has identified different themes within the literature. These include: literature supporting e-books as a medium; other literature that presents some disadvantages of e-books; some material that defends traditional books; and a single source that suggests how the two might co-exist. For various reasons, Andrew rejected a number of sources from his original selection. Table 9.1 illustrates the themes that Andrew has identified in the source material; he has grouped similar aspects together to help him structure his discussion.

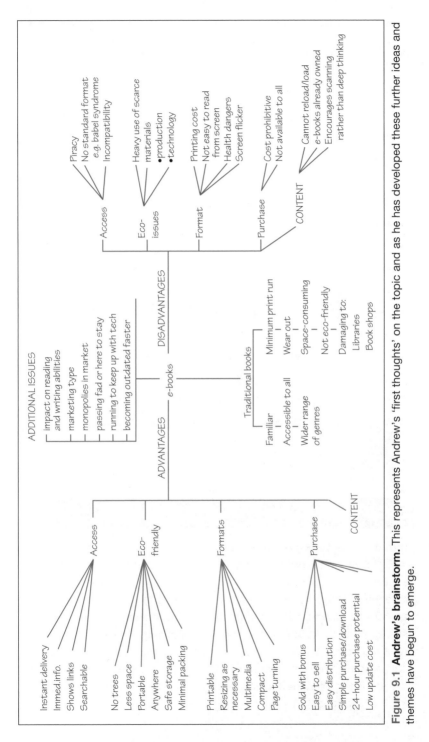

Figure 9.1 Andrew's brainstorm. This represents Andrew's 'first thoughts' on the topic and as he has developed these further ideas and themes have begun to emerge.

Example 9.1 Selection of 15 resources that Andrew sourced. Note that the entries are arranged in alphabetical order by author and represent what might become the draft reference list.

Title

Abrahams, I., 2011, *Resolving the e-differences for the digital age*. Nairn: Nimrod Publishing

Axon, T., 2010. *Green electronics*. Skye: Island Press

Carnaby, J., 2009. *The eye of the beholder*. London: Foley Press

Deutsch, O., 2011. *Old books for booklovers*. Bonn: Teutonia Press, page 10

e-marketing Journal 2010, vol. 3.2, 19–23

Guthrie, A., *The Scotsman*, 2 September 2008

International Media Journal 2009, vol. 1, 67–75

Ludd, N., 2011. *Before you turn the page*. Leicester: Old World Press

Mauser, M., 2012. *e-technology as a study aid*. Godmanchester: Clockwork Press

Peel, P., 2009. *e-books and e-readers: tools for dyslexics*. Greenwich: Ely Press

Quirk, V., 2009. *Travelling with e-books*. Folkestone: Gaskin Press

Sim, P., 2008. *Closed books*. Gateshead: Tyne Press

Smith, D., 2008. *e-data in a digital age*. Nice: Franck Press

Sweeney, T., 2007. *The new library*. New Jersey: World Press

Thom, T. and Dick, H., 2011. *The loss of critical thinking*. Winnipeg: New World Press

---

ORGANISING BY FUNCTION

From the selected literature Andrew then extracts sections that he wants to use to support his discussion and has noted *verbatim* sections that he will cite by quoting, summarising or paraphrasing. For each of these he has tentatively identified the function that these ideas might perform in his discussion. These functions include asserting, conjecturing, describing, exemplifying, expressing opinion, providing data and reporting opinion or findings. Table 9.2 shows each of the 12 *verbatim* chunks of text and the corresponding function that indicates the role that the content of these items could play in his writing.

Table 9.1 Key ideas identified from each text organised by theme. Andrew decided not to use the last four books on the list because they were irrelevant to his task; the remaining sources are grouped reflecting similar themes.

Original text	Title
Advantages of traditional books in critical thought	Thom, T. and Dick, H., 2011. *The loss of critical thinking.* Winnipeg: New World Press
Appeal of traditional books	Deutsch, O., 2011. *Old books for booklovers.* Bonn: Teutonia Press, page 10
Impact of e-books on libraries	Smith, D., 2008. *e-data in a digital age.* Nice: Franck Press
Advantages of e-books to students	Quirk, V., 2009. *Travelling with e-books.* Folkestone: Gaskin Press
Multimodality and e-books	Mauser, M., 2012. *e-technology as a study aid.* Godmanchester: Clockwork Press
Communicating among e-providers	Abrahams, I., 2011. *Resolving the e-differences for the digital age.* Nairn: Nimrod Publishing
Disadvantages of e-books	Peel, P., 2009. *e-books and e-readers: tools for dyslexics.* Greenwich: Ely Press
Disadvantages of e-books	Sim, P., 2008. *Closed books.* Gateshead: Tyne Press
Disadvantages of e-books	Ludd, N., 2011. *Before you turn the page.* Leicester: Old World Press
Green lobby divisions	Axon, T., 2010. *Green electronics.* Skye: Island Press
Green lobby perceptions	Axon, T., 2010. *Green electronics.* Skye: Island Press
Alternative debate	Guthrie, A., *The Scotsman*, 2 September 2008
✗ **Advantage of e-books**	Carnaby, J., 2009. *The eye of the beholder.* London: Foley Press
✗ **Advantages of e-books over traditional books**	Sweeney, T., 2007. *The new library.* New Jersey: World Press
✗ **Advantages of e-technology**	*e-marketing Journal* 2010, vol. 3.2, 19–23
✗ **The Press and e-technology**	*International Media Journal* 2009, vol. 1, 67–75

Table 9.2 **Organising the extracts by function.** For the purposes of this book, the content of the texts is shown as direct quotation; the intention would not be to integrate them into the full text as quotations. Here they are listed according to function as defined in **Chapter 5**.

Original text	Function
1 Advantages of traditional books in critical thought Traditional books stimulate critical thinking; e-books encourage scanning rather than assimilation. (Thom, T. and Dick, H., 2011. *The loss of critical thinking.* Winnipeg: New World Press)	**Supporting opinion** pro traditional books **Contrasting**
2 Appeal of traditional books 'smell of leather-bound volumes and the tactile delight of flicking through the pages of a hard copy book cannot be replicated by a piece of plastic' (Deutsch, O., 2011. *Old books for booklovers.* Bonn: Teutonia Press, page 10)	**Asserting**
3 Advantages of e-books to students The convenience of the e-reader and the accompanying e-books is marked by portability and economy of size. (Quirk, V., 2009. *Travelling with e-books.* Folkestone: Gaskin Press)	**Describing** advantages
4 Green lobby perceptions The green lobby sees anything that saves the world's rainforests as saving the future, hence, they view the replacement and ultimate demise of the traditional paper-based book by e-versions as a good thing. (Axon, T., 2010. *Green electronics.* Skye: Island Press)	**Stating opinion** pro e-books **Conjecturing**
5 Multimodality and e-books The 24/7 access and the multimodal features that enable the reader to skim through chapters, taking notes if they wish, and then storing the entirety until next required presents students, in particular, with advantageous functions that are time-saving and cost-effective. (Mauser, M., 2012. *e-technology as a study aid.* Godmanchester: Clockwork Press)	**Asserting opinion** pro e-books
6 Disadvantages of e-books The problem about e-books is that they are simply not nice to read; they are clumsy to hold and remove the comfort of sitting down to enjoy reading in a relaxed way. The e-book is simply another stress-inducing screen to be worshipped. (Ludd, N., 2011. *Before you turn the page.* Leicester: Old World Press)	**Reporting** defects **Asserting** viewpoint
7 Communicating among e-providers Producers of e-readers and e-books need to recognize that, in seeking to isolate their own products to achieve customer loyalty, they will simply alienate their customers for whom the lack of interchangeability and standardization simply emphasizes the e-Babel issues and increases alienation. (Abrahams, I., 2011. *Resolving the e-differences for the digital age.* Nairn: Nimrod Publishing)	**Conjecturing** re disadvantages of e-books

Key:

☐ Advantages of traditional books   ☐ Disadvantages of e-books

■ Advantages of e-books   ■ Neutral position

Table 9.2 *continued*

Original text	Function
8 Disadvantages of e-books The on-screen flickering image is painful to people with eye-sight problems and may be unhelpful to those with perception of the printed word, for example, people who are dyslexic. (Peel, P., 2009. *e-books and e-readers: tools for dyslexics.* Greenwich: Ely Press)	**Expressing opinion** **Exemplifying**
9 Disadvantages of e-books As few as 50,000 books are estimated to be in circulation and no indication of how these can be generally accessed except by e-readers that are specific to one particular bookseller and the only books that can be downloaded are those on that bookseller's catalogue. (Sim, P., 2008. *Closed books.* Gateshead: Tyne Press)	**Providing** supporting data **Reporting** negative implications
10 Green lobby divisions The green community may find that their principles are compromised because, in accepting the adoption of the electronic book they are simultaneously contributing to wastage of scarce mineral and other resources involved in the manufacture of yet another electronic device and the creation of even more electronic 'debris'. (Axon, T., 2010. *Green electronics.* Skye: Island Press)	**Reporting** negative implications
11 Alternative debate 'it [the e-book] should be looked at as an alternative … one doesn't necessarily herald the decline of the other…'. Guthrie, A., *The Scotsman*, 2 September 2008.	**Expressing** neutral opinion
12 Impact of e-books on libraries Libraries as we know them may degenerate to become depositories of pre-electronic material that will become increasingly fragile until disposal is the only sensible route. The days of the traditional librarian are numbered; the only option is to seek reinvention as pedlars of the e-word as custodians of the digital archives. (Smith, D., 2008. *e-data in a digital age.* Nice: Franck Press)	**Conjecturing** **Describing** cause and effect relationship

EVOLVING THE LANGUAGE STRUCTURES

Andrew has created an order of using the selected source material that follows a classic model of presenting argument. Table 9.3 shows the chosen order following the numbering system used in Table 9.2. In the third column, he has listed the attitude verbs he intends to use to report each item. Note that he has chosen to adopt the simple past tense to report the work of his chosen authors.

Table 9.3 **Order in which Andrew structures the evidence as part of his wider discussion.** The structure that Andrew has decided to follow allows him to draw in supporting evidence in each section of this paper, that is, in the introduction, main body and conclusion.

Original text	Function	How used
3 Advantages to students The convenience of the e-reader and the accompanying e-books is marked by portability and economy of size. (Quirk, V., 2009. *Travelling with e-books*. Folkestone: Gaskin Press)	**Describing** advantages	Quirk (2009) commented that …
6 Disadvantages of e-books The problem about e-books is that they are simply not nice to read; they are clumsy to hold and remove the comfort of sitting down to enjoy reading in a relaxed way. The e-book is simply another stress-inducing screen to be worshipped. (Ludd, N., 2011. *Before you turn the page*. Leicester: Old World Press)	**Reporting** defects **Asserting** viewpoint	Information prominent citation
4 Green lobby perceptions The green lobby sees anything that saves the world's rainforests as saving the future, hence, they view the replacement and ultimate demise of the traditional paper-based book by e-versions as a good thing. (Axon, T., 2010. *Green electronics. Skye:* Island Press)	**Stating opinion** pro e-books **Conjecturing**	Axon (2010) observed that …
5 Multimodality and e-books The 24/7 access and the multimodal features that enable the reader to skim through chapters, taking notes if they wish, and then storing the entirety until next required presents students, in particular, with advantageous functions that are time-saving and cost-effective. (Mauser, M., 2012. *e-technology as a study aid.* Godmanchester: Clockwork Press)	**Asserting** opinion pro e-books	Mauser (2012) claimed that …
7 Communicating among e-providers Producers of e-readers and e-books need to recognize that, in seeking to isolate their own products to achieve customer loyalty, they will simply alienate their customers for whom the lack of interchangeability and standardization simply emphasizes the e-Babel issues and increases alienation. (Abrahams, I., 2011. *Resolving the e-differences for the digital age.* Nairn: Nimrod Publishing)	**Conjecturing** re disadvantages of e-books	Defined by Abrahams (2011) as …
9 Disadvantages of e-books As few as 50,000 books are estimated to be in circulation and no indication of how these can be generally accessed except by e-readers that are specific to one particular bookseller and the only books that can be downloaded are those on that bookseller's catalogue. (Sim, P., 2008. *Closed books.* Gateshead: Tyne Press)	**Providing supporting data** **Reporting** negative implications	Sim (2008) estimated that …

	Reporting	
10 Green lobby divisions The green community may find that their principles are compromised because, in accepting the adoption of the electronic book they are simultaneously contributing to wastage of scarce mineral and other resources involved in the manufacture of yet another electronic device and the creation of even more electronic 'debris'. (Axon, T., 2010. *Green electronics*. Skye: Island Press)	Reporting negative implications	... that Axon (2010) characterized as ...
8 Disadvantages of e-books The on-screen flickering image is painful to people with eye-sight problems and may be unhelpful to those with perception of the printed word, for example, people who are dyslexic. (Peel, P., 2009. *e-books and e-readers: tools for dyslexics*. Greenwich: Ely Press)	Expressing opinion Exemplifying	Information prominent citation
1 Advantages of traditional books in critical thought Traditional books stimulate critical thinking; e-books encourage scanning rather than assimilation. (Thom, T. and Dick, H., 2011. *The loss of critical thinking*. Winnipeg: New World Press)	Supporting opinion pro traditional books Contrasting	Thom and Dick (2011) averred that ...
12 Impact of e-books on libraries Libraries as we know them may degenerate to become depositories of pre-electronic material that will become increasingly fragile until disposal is the only sensible route. The days of the traditional librarian are numbered; the only option is to seek reinvention as pedlars of the e-word as custodians of the digital archives. (Smith, D., 2008. *e-data in a digital age*. Nice: Franck Press)	Conjecturing Describing cause and effect relationship	Smith (2008) surmised that ...
2 Appeal of traditional books 'smell of leather-bound volumes and the tactile delight of flicking through the pages of a hard copy book cannot be replicated by a piece of plastic' (Deutsch, O., 2011. *Old books for booklovers*. Bonn: Teutonia Press, page 10)	Asserting	... traditionalists such as Deutsch (2011) argue that ...
11 Alternative debate 'it [the e-book] should be looked at as an alternative...one doesn't necessarily herald the decline of the other...' (Guthrie, A., *The Scotsman*, 2 September 2008)	Expressing neutral opinion	Guthrie (2008) presented the view that ...

Key:

☐ Advantages of traditional books ▢ Advantages of e-books ☐ Disadvantages of e-books ▨ Neutral position

INTEGRATING CITATIONS INTO THE WORK

Following a model similar to that outlined in **Chapter 5**, Andrew has written a draft of his paper (Example 9.2(a)) which includes the 11 citations that he had identified as most relevant to his text. Note that he has drawn two excerpts from one of these resources.

To illustrate the difference that citation makes to a text, Example 9.2(b) shows the text structured in the same way and with some slightly different wording since there are no citations. If submitted, such a paper would not be regarded as having academic merit for a number of reasons:

- it lacks any evidence of background reading;
- it makes assertions without any supporting evidence;
- it makes assertions but without any reference to authorities;
- it overtly plagiarises by taking words directly from the text; and
- it gives some numerical information but does not source this.

Example 9.2(a) presents a discussion that clearly demonstrates research and critical thinking, whereas Example 9.2(b) appears as a series of unsupported opinions. It would seem to have been written by someone who has never engaged with the current thinking on the topic or even consulted anything more than the popular press, but has simply drawn on personal experience and opinion. The text in Example 9.2(b) would, therefore, not receive a good grade.

Plagiarism checking services

While there are many organisations on the web that offer plagiarism checking services, it is not worth engaging with such services. They are just that – services, and ones for which you have to pay a lot of money. They are not about helping you learn or even about getting good grades. These organisations are not regulated and there is no certainty that what they offer will provide a professional appraisal of your work. Many of these sites are non-UK based and so what they offer as feedback on your work may result in something that is not acceptable in terms of style or content to meet British standards of higher education.

Example 9.2(a) Andrew's text *with* attribution. This text shows each citation and the associated 'attitude' verb which Andrew has used to cite fact and present opinion and conjecture (see **Ch 4**).

E-books are novel and alluring with a well-publicised supporting technology. The book concept has not changed much since Gutenberg's printing press in the fifteenth century and the hard copy traditional book has its champions. Nevertheless, the exciting concept of a hand-held 200 megabyte electronic reservoir containing the equivalent of 160 novels – the e-book – holds attraction that the bibliophile may find difficult to resist. **Quirk (2009)** commented that there are obvious advantages of space and portability but traditionalists contend that the e-book concept has inherent disadvantages **(Ludd, 2011)**. This paper examines the opposing viewpoints and also draws some comparisons with traditional books.

E-books offer a facility that other printed formats cannot emulate. Perhaps the strongest advantage lies in the ease of access and availability plus simple purchase procedures. In a few moments readers can choose online and take immediate delivery of the book. Instant access to literature makes information available with the capacity to search and follow in-built electronic links. Purchasing incentives offering bonus deals such as books costing less than one pound have contributed to the positive perception of e-book merchandise. Currently, downloadable updates have been maintained at low cost as a further attractive incentive.

To their credit, e-books have a strong 'green' profile. Marketing and distribution costs are pared to a minimum reducing use of paper needed for traditional books and expensive distribution networks. Their delivery requires neither packaging nor a significant 'carbon footprint' in transport costs. As **Axon (2010)** observed, ecologists see the paperless e-book as saving rainforests by making the paper-based book redundant.

Format possibilities offer further advantages; e-book format can be enhanced by multimedia possibilities including film and audio functions. Typically, e-books comprise a clickable contents page and have a page-turning facility with some e-readers offering a bulkier 'double page' option. The electronic versions can be modified in terms of font choice and point resizing. Full text can also be printed if necessary from the personal printer.

Expensive storage facilities are no longer required in the e-book world. Portability and size of e-readers and electronic storage of e-books mean that bulky storage and preservation needs are negated immediately. Consequently, e-book users no longer need to be burdened by large volumes of books thus giving the e-book an overriding advantage over traditional books.

The content of e-books can present a number of genres that allows the reader to pursue a range of interest in fiction and non-fiction areas. **Mauser (2012)** claimed that books can be accessed at any time and their e-format also has appeal because the content can be safely stored even with additional information. He suggests, for example, that the ability to navigate across chapters, skim read, book-mark and annotate enables students to make and store notes and books together which is an attractive option to students with limited time.

Nonetheless, e-book technology is not without its critics and the themes identified as strengths also present some negative dimensions in the e-book versus traditional book debate.

A key criticism of the e-book concept is that it is hardware and software dependent. Defined by **Abrahams (2011)** as the e-Babel problem, hardware–software dependency

Continued overleaf

Example 9.2(a) *continued*

highlights the lack of standardisation so that content purchased for one application is not necessarily compatible with rival e-reader hardware.This has come about because accessibility, it is argued, is defined by the vendors of e-readers. **Sim (2008)** estimated that at that time there were approximately 50,000 e-books available in circulation, but control over access to these books is maintained by the booksellers selling e-readers that will only provide the reading function to allow books bought through their outlets.

A point which is less frequently acknowledged by the e-book vendor is that even e-books are dependent on the imagination and hard work of authors so, despite claims of low overhead costs by e-publishers, authors still need to be paid for their labour whether their work is destined for the e-book or the traditional book. That said, ease of online access opens opportunities for e-piracy which can mean 'raids' on particular titles or genres with no compensation to author or publisher. Thus, this threat affects not only e-merchants but also those under whose copyright the resource is originally marketed.

In terms of green credentials and low carbon cost, the e-book case is damaged by what **Axon (2010)** characterised as its contribution to electronic 'debris' through heavy use of scarce materials in the manufacture of the hardware. For students, while the concept might be attractive, it may remain academic as the requirement of a basic outlay of anything between £100–£200 makes the initial outlay expense prohibitive.

While it is claimed that the potential for variation in on-screen format is an asset, one of the most powerful criticisms is that reading on-screen is, for many people, a painful activity and unhelpful for those with certain unseen disabilities such as dyslexia (**Peel, 2007**), particularly. Less is said about the ease with which people can read the 'static' printed book. Furthermore, as critics of the e-book, **Thom and Dick (2011)** averred that

> the 'skim and dip' facility of the electronic medium promotes a tendency towards a short attention span when reading and is a serious factor in diminishing the critical appraisal that educationalists argue is only truly exercised when readers read text sequentially.
>
> Thom and Dick, 2011, p. 23

As noted, bonus offers with some e-readers come with 100 or so 'free' titles. Until non-fiction titles become more readily available in e-book format, this diminishes the functionality of the device, particularly for students, if academic titles are not as readily available as books being read for pleasure and leisure. However, the number of titles that can be made available very quickly in e-formats diminishes the case for the traditional copy where print-runs may be as low as 1,000 thus limiting sales and distribution. **Smith (2008)** surmised that a reduction in the printing and distribution of hard copy books may mean that in time, libraries – and librarians – may become obsolete. If they survive it will undoubtedly be in a different guise – perhaps as purveyors of e-literature.

Despite such prophecies, traditionalists such as **Deutsch (2009, p10)** argue that 'the smell of leather-bound volumes and the tactile delight of flicking through the pages of a hard copy book cannot be replicated by a piece of plastic'. Whether that is a view shared by the e-lobby, for the time being, the debate will continue to rage and yet **Guthrie (2008)** presented the view that 'it [the e-book] should be looked at as an alternative…one doesn't necessarily herald the decline of the other …'. [*1117 words*]

Example 9.2(b) Andrew's text *without* attribution. This version of Andrew's text shows no citations. While it conveys some sense of being well-enough argued, there is no evidence of reading or of evaluation of the literature.

E-books are novel and alluring with a well-publicised supporting technology. The concept of the book has not changed much since Gutenberg's creation of the printing press in the fifteenth century and the hard copy traditional book has its champions. Nevertheless, the exciting concept of a hand-held 200 megabyte electronic reservoir containing the equivalent of 160 novels – the e-book – holds attraction that the bibliophile may find difficult to resist. However, there are obvious advantages of space and portability but traditionalists argue that the e-book concept has inherent disadvantages. This paper examines the opposing viewpoints and also draws some comparisons with traditional books.

E-books offer a facility that other printed formats cannot emulate. Perhaps the strongest advantage lies in the ease of accessibility enabled by round-the-clock availability and simple purchase procedures. In the space of a few moments readers can make their choice online and take immediate delivery of their book. Instant access to the literature – fiction or non-fiction – makes information available with the capacity to search and follow in-built electronic links. Purchasing incentives offering bonus deals such as books costing less than one pound have contributed to the positive perception of e-book merchandise. Currently, downloadable updates have been maintained at low cost as a further attractive incentive.

To their credit, e-books have a strong 'green' profile. Marketing and distribution costs are pared to a minimum reducing use of paper needed for traditional books and expensive distribution networks. Their delivery requires neither packaging nor a significant 'carbon footprint' in transport costs. Ecologists see the paperless e-book as saving rainforests by making the paper-based book redundant.

The format possibilities offer further advantages. For example, the e-book format can be enhanced by multimedia possibilities including film and audio functions. Typically, e-books comprise a clickable contents page and have a page-turning or flipping facility with some e-readers offering a bulkier 'double page' option. For those with sight difficulties, the electronic version can be modified in terms of font choice and point resizing. Full text can also be printed if necessary from the personal printer.

Expensive storage facilities are no longer required in the e-book world. Portability and size of e-readers and electronic storage of e-books mean that bulky storage and preservation needs are negated immediately. Consequently, e-book users no longer need to be burdened by large volumes of books thus giving the e-book an overriding advantage over traditional books.

The content of e-books can present a number of genres that allows the reader to pursue a range of interest in fiction and non-fiction areas. Books can be accessed at any time and their e-format also has appeal because the content can be safely stored even with additional information. For example, the ability to navigate across chapters aids skim reading, book-marking and annotating allows students to make and store notes and books together which is an attractive option to students with limited time.

Continued overleaf

Example 9.2(b) *continued*

Nonetheless, e-book technology is not without its critics and the themes identified as strengths also present some negative dimensions in the e-book versus traditional book debate.

A key criticism of the e-book concept is that it is hardware and software dependent. Sometimes referred to as the e-Babel problem, it highlights the lack of standardisation so that content purchased for one application is not necessarily compatible with rival e-reader hardware. This lack of standardisation is a serious disincentive to people wishing to embrace the technology to its fullest extent. This has come about because accessibility, it is argued, is defined by the vendors of e-readers. Estimates claim that there are approximately 50,000 e-books available in circulation, but control over access to these books is maintained by the booksellers who are selling e-readers that will only provide the reading function to allow books bought through their outlets.

That said, ease of access opens opportunities for e-piracy which can mean 'raids' on particular titles or genres. This threat affects not only e-merchants but also those under whose copyright the resource is originally marketed.

In terms of green credentials and low carbon cost, the e-book position is damaged by the toll of the contribution to electronic 'debris' through heavy use of scarce materials in the manufacture of the e-reader hardware. For students, while the concept might be attractive, it may remain academic as the requirement of a basic outlay of anything between £100–£200 makes the initial outlay expense prohibitive.

While it is claimed that the potential for variation in on-screen format, one of the most powerful criticisms is that reading on-screen is, for many people, a painful activity. Less is said about the ease with which people can read the 'static' printed book. Furthermore, the presentation of material on screen as provided by e-books is said to encourage skim reading rather than in-depth analysis possible when reading a hard copy book.

As noted, bonus offers with some e-readers come with 100 or so 'free' titles, until non-fiction titles become more readily available in e-book format, this diminishes the functionality of the device if academic titles are not as readily available as books being read for pleasure and leisure. However, the number of titles that can be made available very quickly in e-formats diminishes the case for the traditional copy where print-runs may be as low as 1,000 thus limiting sales and distribution. A reduction in the printing and distribution of hard copy books may mean that in time, libraries – and librarians – may become obsolete. If they survive it will undoubtedly be in a different guise – perhaps as purveyors of e-literature.

A point which is less frequently acknowledged by the e-book vendor is that even e-books are dependent on the imagination and hard work of authors so, despite claims of low overhead costs, authors still need to be paid for their labour whether to the e-book or the traditional book publisher. Traditionalists argue that the smell of leather-bound volumes and the tactile delight of flicking through the pages of a hard copy book cannot be replicated by a piece of plastic. For the time being, the debate will continue to rage and yet the e-book should be looked at as an alternative … one doesn't necessarily herald the decline of the other. [*1024 words*]

COMPILING THE REFERENCE LIST

The reference list for this work would follow the format of the Harvard style. The list is shown in Example 9.3.

Example 9.3 Reference list for Andrew's paper. This list represents all the sources cited in Andrew's text. It follows the Harvard style **(Ch 13)**.

Abrahams, I., 2011. *Resolving the e-differences for the digital age.* Nairn: Nimrod Publishing

Axon, T., 2010. *Green electronics.* Skye: Island Press

Deutsch, O., 2011. *Old books for booklovers.* Bonn: Teutonia Press, page 10

Guthrie, A. *The Scotsman*, 2 September 2008

Ludd, N., 2011. *Before you turn the page.* Leicester: Old World Press

Mauser, M., 2012. *e-technology as a study aid.* Godmanchester: Clockwork Press

Peel, P., 2009. *e-books and e-readers: tools for dyslexics.* Greenwich: Ely Press

Quirk, V., 2009. *Travelling with e-books.* Folkestone: Gaskin Press

Sim, P., 2008. *Closed books.* Gateshead: Tyne Press

Smith, D., 2008. *e-data in a digital age.* Nice: Franck Press

Thom, T. and Dick, H., 2011. *The loss of critical thinking.* Winnipeg: New World Press

PRACTICAL TIPS FOR REFLECTING ON THE PROCESSES OF CITATION

Choose your own brainstorming method. This need not be done in the 'mind-map' format shown here. Some people dislike mind-maps intensely because they simply do not fit with their learning style while others love them. Feel free to devise your own method, for example, using thematic lists, bullet points, flow charts or tables.

Use the specialist services in your library to find out more about the resources in your subject area. As noted in **Chapter 4**, your library website may provide information about specialist search engines or repositories of books that will help your literature search. In addition, librarians have a wealth of understanding of the material they provide and if you find that you are not being particularly successful in finding material, then do ask for help.

9.1 Compare the use of attitude verbs. The case study example uses a number of attitude verbs to report the ideas of others. Identify those used in the case study and consult Table 6.1 to ascertain whether any of the verbs listed there could substitute for the verbs in the text. This will help you to become more familiar with the options available to you and encourage you not to use the same structure all the time. It will also mean that you become used to considering carefully the function that you are wishing to fulfil in your writing.

9.2 Find out what specialist services your library offers. If you visit the library website, you will find a number of areas that will help you – access to online dictionaries and encyclopaedias, to specialist search engines, and to specialist journals for which your library has an institutional subscription. If you do not understand what these involve, then, again, ask a librarian to explain.

9.3 Review the idea of critical thinking explained in Chapter 1. With this in mind, review the ways in which Andrew's essay has demonstrated his critical thinking and reflect on how you employ your critical thinking abilities in your own writing.

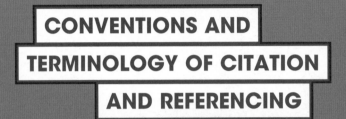

CONVENTIONS AND TERMINOLOGY OF CITATION AND REFERENCING

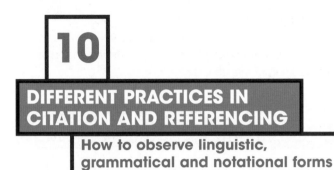

10

DIFFERENT PRACTICES IN CITATION AND REFERENCING

How to observe linguistic, grammatical and notational forms

As you will now be aware from earlier chapters, there is more to referencing than using the correct punctuation and formatting within the text of your work. Your reading will have led you to sources that may have used citation and referencing styles that are unfamiliar to you and that may seem nonsensical or even old-fashioned. However, learning about some of the idiosyncrasies you may encounter will help you to understand them and also to elicit the information that you need to integrate citations from this material into your own work.

KEY TOPICS

→ What influences choice of citation and referencing style?

→ Categories of style that are most commonly used

→ Footnotes and abbreviations

→ Bibliography or Reference List?

→ The context for citation – language issues

KEY TERMS

Active voice   Ampersand   Parenthetical   Passive voice
Personal pronouns

There are many systems that are used in the world of academic writing and publication and you will not need all of the information in this chapter for each of them. However, to make sense of the various referencing styles, it may be helpful to know that a number of factors govern the choice and interpretation practised in different subject areas and even amongst colleagues within an academic department. This means that students and researchers may be exposed to different citation and referencing styles, some of which are identical to or derive from a variety of the more widely used styles. Before you consult five of these styles in the following chapters, certain points relating to their interpretation are outlined in this chapter.

WHAT INFLUENCES CHOICE OF CITATION AND REFERENCING STYLE?

A myriad of organisations are in the position of imposing distinctive citation and referencing styles on those who publish under their auspices. The reason for this is to establish standardisation in style, notably in the following areas:

- **International and national standards.** In the English-speaking world a number of organisations have created their own 'in-house' style to achieve standardisation. In some instances, these relate to more universally used referencing styles (although there may have been minor modifications, usually to the punctuation). Table 10.1 lists a number of organisations outside the academic world whose standards may be used in the source material you use.

- **Publishing houses.** Companies who publish in the academic field standardise their publications to keep costs down. Hence, their authors are provided with guidelines to which they must adhere exactly if they wish their material to be published. This applies to academic textbooks, journals and periodicals.

- **Discipline-specific practices.** In some disciplines, there are very strict practices for referencing. In Law, for example, how cases are cited and referenced is important to the clarity of an argument; in Politics, citation of government papers and international documents is similarly important. English literature and certain branches of History follow very singular practices and you will be taught these as part of your course. Generally, if any rule of thumb exists, there will be exceptions to it and so it is advisable to check your course handbook or guidelines.

- **Professional bodies and learned societies**. These organisations often produce journals and periodicals for the dissemination of research developments. Consequently, distinctive sets of citation and referencing styles have evolved to become the standard for these disciplines. For example, in the field of Psychology, the standard is that defined by the American Psychological Association

Table 10.1 Conventions and terminology of citation and referencing styles. Measures to achieve standardisation in referencing and citation practices operate at international and regional levels.

1. International organisations	Further information at:
International Organization for Standardization	Information and documentation – Guidelines for bibliographic references and citations of information resources. *www.iso.org*
2. Regional organisations	**Further information at:**
European Union (EU)	*English Style Guide* defines the correct citation of EU documents (*ec.europa.eu/ translation/english/guidelines/documents/ styleguide_english_dgt_en.pdf*)
Australia	*http://australia.gov.au/publications/style-manual*
Canada	No national guide, but standards for legal citation exist as follows: *Canadian Guide to Uniform Legal Citation, 7th Edition/ Manuel Canadien de la Référence Juridique, 7e* (*www.carswell.com*) since no formal Canadian guide exists for legal citation. Note that different discipline associations prescribe their chosen style.
United Kingdom	• British Standards Institution. *Information and documentation – Guidelines for bibliographic references and citations to information resources.* London: BSI, 2010 (BS ISO 690). • British Standards Institution. *Recommendations for citing and referencing published materials.* London: BSI, 1990 (BS 5605). • British Standards Institution. *Recommendations for citation of unpublished documents.* London: BSI, 1983 (BS 6371). Note that there have been long gaps between consecutive BS publications and that the 2010 version applies only to information resources; otherwise the 1990 version applies. Economic and Social Data Service (*www.esds.ac.uk/ international/access/citing.asp*)
United States of America	For citation of legal documents: • *The Blue Book: A Uniform System of Citation ® for US Legal Citations* (*www.legalbluebook*) • *ALWD Citation Manual* (*www.alwd.org*). Outside the discipline of law, other disciplines follow subject related guidelines.

(APA) (see **Ch 11**). In certain areas of Medicine, the style followed is that of the *British Medical Journal*.

- **Your lecturer or supervisor.** Academics may seem particularly intransigent on the subject of citation and referencing style. This may arise from their own need to suit the publishing requirements of the journals in which they themselves seek publication or because they are performing an editorial role for a journal and so they assume that prescription as their 'default' citation style. Alternatively, they may have to follow an agreed departmental norm or they may follow a style that is the professional style as dictated by a learned society or a professional association. This may all seem rather arcane and strange, but, since academics are contractually bound to undertake and publish research, the need to follow a consistent style applicable to a range of publishing possibilities can save considerable time – even with the advent of electronic referencing systems, moving an entire document from one format to another is extremely time-consuming.

> ✔ When your course requires you to adopt different citation and referencing styles because you have 'crossed' subject boundaries, you need to be alert to the fact that you will have to alter your citation and referencing system to meet the different guidelines. For example, students studying Politics may have to follow the Harvard Style but because they may also concurrently be studying a course on European Law which uses the specialist citation conventions of a School of Law, they will have to be aware of, learn and observe both systems.

CATEGORIES OF STYLE THAT ARE MOST COMMONLY USED

In the UK, the British Standard system provides some guidance on bibliographical referencing and these may be available via your library. However, in practice, as noted above, universities tend to adhere to styles that are the norm for their disciplines or the departments within their institutions or publishers of academic journals. There are few instances of institutions opting for a single style that will be used across disciplines. For simplicity, the systems described in this book can be classified into the following groups:

- **Author name/date** (sometimes called parenthetical) systems are used in the social sciences and humanities as well as the natural sciences. However, there are significant differences about layout and language related to these and you can view these in Part 5.

  Example: *'Campbell and Hutton (2012) suggested that ...'*
- **Numeric/footnote plus reference/bibliography list** is used in scientific styles to give information in a numbered footnote about authorship on the same page as the citation first appears. Numbering may be full-size or superscript.

  Example: *'In the view of Campbell and Hutton*[15]*...*
- **Author name/page number** used in some disciplines within the humanities and includes the Modern Languages Association (MLA) style.

  Example: *'In the view of Campbell and Hutton (133) observed that ...'*
- **Numeric system** (sometimes called the numbered or scientific system) and used most commonly in the sciences. It would be inadvisable to use this system unless you have been told to do so. The number relates to the number of the reference in the reference list.

  Example: *'In the view of Campbell and Hutton (15) ...'* or *'In the view of Campbell and Hutton*[15]*...'*

Chapters 11–15 provide examples of five commonly used styles:

- **American Psychological Association (APA) Style** is used in both sciences and social sciences. It follows a name/date style.
- **Chicago Style** (sometimes called Turabian because of its close relationship to the work of Kate Turabian who developed her system in the 1970s) is used in the scientific community and social sciences where a scientific approach has been followed. It follows a numeric/footnote style.
- **Harvard Style** which was not named after the US Harvard University but after John Harvard, an American clergyman, who bequeathed his library of books to Cambridge College, Massachusetts in 1637. This is one of the most commonly used styles and is accepted in disciplines across social and life sciences as well as in engineering. It follows the author/date style.
- **Modern Languages Association (MLA) Style**, as its name suggests, is designed to suit disciplines in the humanities. It follows the author/page number style.

- **Vancouver Style** is most commonly used in medical and related fields. It follows the numeric (scientific) style.

FOOTNOTES AND ABBREVIATIONS

Since footnotes are used in some styles of citation, it is important to confirm your understanding of some of the terms and abbreviations that are used in these formats. Table 10.2 provides a list of the more commonly used. Example 10.1 exemplifies and explains their use in a reference list.

Table 10.2 **Use of abbreviations in citations and referencing.** The following words, phrases and abbreviations are frequently used in citations, including footnotes, in textbooks and academic journals. Most good dictionaries explain their meaning.

Abbreviation	Language	Meaning or interpretation
& (ampersand)	Latin	'and' but note only used in certain styles
cf.	Latin	compare with
ch./chs.	English	chapter/chapters
ed.	English	editor/editions
et al.	Latin	and others
ff.	Latin	following
ibid.	Latin	in the same place
loc. cit.	Latin	the same page as previous citation for the same work
MSS	English	manuscripts
op. cit.	Latin	as earlier reference to the same work but not the immediately previous reference
passim	Latin	throughout
p. or pp.	English	page or pages
sic	Latin	'thus', that is, as printed possibly erroneously in original
vide	Latin	see (in a book or reference work seek that word)
viz.	Latin	namely

Example 10.1 **Use of abbreviations in citations and referencing.** The footnotes relate to a text on critical thinking in university education. This footnoting style is typical of a numbered referencing system. The footnotes may appear at the bottom of the relevant page or as a list at the end of the work.

Example of numbered footnote list	Points interpreting corresponding footnote
1. Beattie, I.M., 2010 *Critical Thinking at University* pp. 25–40.	1. Title in italics followed by page numbers.
2. *ibid*, p. 40.	2. *ibid.*, p. 40 means the immediately previous reference on page 40.
3. *ibid*.	3. *ibid.* means the previous reference on same page as in number 2.
4. Jenkins, P., *et al.* 2004, *Evidence and Analysis.*	4. *et al.* implies written by three or more authors; details in relevant reference list.
5. Beattie, *op. cit.* p. 35.	5. Last reference to this author (footnote 1) but specifically on page 35.
6. Higgins, P., 2008, 'Quality writing in university learning' *Journal of University Education* vol. 11, p. 30.	6. Title of article or chapter (standard print within inverted commas) within journal (printed in italics) followed by volume and page numbers.
7. Forestier, R.R., (ed.), 2001, 'The perfect answer: analysis and evidential support' *Logic, Creativity and Critique in Student Writing.*	7. Forestier is the editor (ed.) who wrote a chapter (title in standard font) in the book (in italics).
8. Swift, A., 2010, 'The Analytical Learner' in Craig and Christopher (eds) *Analysis in Classroom Teaching.*	8. Swift wrote a chapter (in inverted commas) in a book edited (eds) by Craig and Christopher, title of book in italics.
9. *ibid.* p. 124.	9. Same as immediately previous reference but on page 124.
10. Cairns, F.M., 2009 *Theories of Critical Thinking for the Educationalist and the Learner. Passim.*	10. Topic relating to the figure 4 is dealt with throughout (*passim*) the work (*passim* is in italics because it is a Latin word).
11. cf. in this connection with the work of N. Parker.	11. Compare with the work of N. Parker. (More information via Google Scholar or Library catalogue.)

BIBLIOGRAPHY OR REFERENCE LIST?

The most fundamental of definitions distinguishing these two terms is that a Bibliography is a list of all the material that has been read in order to prepare a piece of writing, whereas a Reference List comprises only those sources cited in the text. Some disciplines, especially in the arts, opt for the term Bibliography while others prefer the practice of providing only a list of references. However, sometimes the differences are blurred as terms such as 'Works cited' or 'Works consulted' also seem to be preferred in certain disciplines. Again, best to check with your handbook or the relevant academic.

> **i** When you need to cite two or more works published in the same year by the same author, then the usual approach is to use the format Smith 2012a, Smith 2012b, Smith 2012c and so on for the in-text citation and to list them in the reference list in the a, b, c order as in the text. The lower case letter follows the date of publication in the reference list.

THE CONTEXT FOR CITATION – LANGUAGE ISSUES

Particular aspects of language use apply to some of the styles described in Chapters 11–15. For clarity, these are outlined below.

- **Active and passive.** There are conflicting opinions about the use of these two linguistic devices (defined in the Glossary). Some academics and citation systems encourage the use of the active voice: *I gave the results to the statistician.* They argue that this type of expression is more modern, colloquial and clearer to understand. Other academics and citation systems prefer the use of the passive: *Negative results had been interpreted by the statistician to show that ...* (Lythe, 2007). It is argued that this form of expression is more formal and therefore more representative of the serious nature of academic research as it places the emphasis on the action rather than the 'actor' who may not even be mentioned. Some regard the passive as more long-winded while others feel that the active is too familiar and detracts from the objective analysis of the content. The debate is one that will no doubt continue without resolution, but unless you are given a hard and fast ruling, then you can use active and passive as you deem appropriate within the same document. (See also **Ch 6**.)

- **Personal pronouns.** These are defined in the Glossary, but for the purposes of citation, there are two conflicting conventions. One is that the first person singular or plural (I/we) should not be used in academic writing; the other is that these should be encouraged. Clearly, these are frequently interlinked with the use of active/passive voice as explained above. Occasions when 'I' and 'we' are permitted include reporting group effort in a laboratory where all participants make a contribution to a research project or where the task is to write reflectively on a critical incident in nursing, education or social work, for example. The personal pronoun 'you' is not regarded as appropriate for use in the majority of academic texts, unless you have been given explicit instructions permitting this. (See also **Ch 6**.)

PRACTICAL TIPS FOR FOLLOWING CONVENTIONS IN ALTERNATIVE CITATION AND REFERENCING STYLES

Compare any guidelines you have been given with the proclaimed referencing system. Frequently, instructions to writers will claim that the citation and referencing style follows a particular interpretation, for example, the Harvard Style. However, it is important to compare the guidelines as illustrated in any guidance notes you have been given with the identified style since these may not match. This problem arises because people (and organisations) who perhaps have never actually examined the 'official' versions may have modified the style in minor, but sometimes major, respects along the way. Alternatively, guidelines may claim to be unique to the organisation issuing these as 'their' style. In this instance, try to identify the style by name since this can be helpful should you find that the instructions you have been given are lacking, for example, by failing to give direction about how to cite one of the more unusual types of media you wish to use, such as websites.

Understand the nomenclature. Note that the word 'style' is used in different ways. Style can relate to the use of language in a text, therefore a 'Style Guide' will discuss aspects of grammar and language use although there may be passing mention of citation and referencing methods. Style can also be used to refer to a particular method and hence the terms 'style' and 'method' are used interchangeably in the context of citing and referencing systems. Additionally, the expression 'bibliographical referencing style' is also used to refer to such systems. These 'styles' do not generally involve discussion of writing style although there are exceptions to this (APA Style, for example).

Be consistent. Although it may appear to be stating the obvious, ensure that the citation and referencing style you choose to adopt or are obliged to follow is observed consistently throughout a piece of writing. There is no 'mixing' option.

(GO) AND NOW . . .

10.1 Check out style issues at an early stage in the process of your writing. While course handbooks and guidelines for publication may give some guidance on issues of citation convention, they may be less informative on the use of passive *versus* active or the use of first person singular/plural. If these matters are not covered in the written instructions, then it is advisable to discuss these specific points with the relevant academic so that, at the outset, you are aware of their preferences (which might even be their unacknowledged requirements). In this way, you can potentially save yourself (and your supervisor) the inconvenience at a later point of having to 'convert' an entire text to make it compliant with the convention that they wish you to follow.

10.2 Check out a journal in your discipline area. Hard copy or online journals will have some information under a title similar to 'Guidelines to Contributors'. Find a journal within your discipline area and look at this section to analyse how the guideline requirements square (or not) with the instructions you have been given. Be aware that if there are discrepancies between the two, you should follow the guidance you have been given as an individual.

10.3 Reflect on your ability to pay attention to detail. Normally, academics would urge students to avoid always striving for perfection in their search for the ideal answer, and rather they would encourage the production of a good response to their writing task. However, in the case of the citations and corresponding references in your work, you must strive for perfection in that the sources you cite in your text must correspond exactly to the references in your reference list or bibliography.

Academics will not only check that they do, but may ask you direct questions about the source material. If you unintentionally forget to remove a reference from your list after you removed a citation at draft stage, this may leave the impression that the reference list has been 'padded' to make it seem that more extensive reading had been done. Be prepared to allocate time in your planning to allow you time to double-check that the citations and references 'match'.

FIVE REFERENCING STYLES

HOW TO USE THIS SECTION

This section contains information about the use of five styles of citation and referencing:

- American Psychological Association (APA) Style (**Ch 11**)
- Chicago Style (**Ch 12**)
- Harvard Style (**Ch 13**)
- Modern Languages Association (MLA) Style (**Ch 14**)
- Vancouver Style (**Ch 15**)

The evolution of these and the many other styles that exist has contributed to some standardisation in the way that references and in-text citations are organised. The diagram below shows typical components of a Reference List or Bibliographic entry.

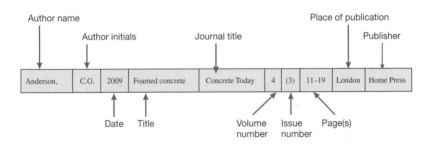

The layout and punctuation differs from one style to another and you will find the specific details in the relevant styles in **Chapters 11–15**.

Styles are constantly developing as researchers and writers turn to an increasingly varied resource bank for their evidence. Thus, covering every possible type of resource that might be used in academic writing would be unrealistic and, inevitably, ever-changing. Therefore, in the following chapters we have used examples of references for hard copy materials as well as the more frequently cited types of electronic materials.

Each of the styles demonstrated contains a sample text that models the style: its use of in-text citation devices and layout of the corresponding Reference List. To emphasise the formatting of citation, the individual references are shown in colour, **thus**. Of course, in the text as you would present it, this colouring would *not* be used.

Models of the use of quotation are also provided for each style. Features that characterise individual styles are also described and include matters of layout, punctuation, and language. Examples of layout are shown for different types of resource material; these examples may differ from one style to another. They have been dictated by the extent to which some styles and the disciplines that follow particular styles have become more inclusive of new technologies.

AMERICAN PSYCHOLOGICAL ASSOCIATION (APA) STYLE

The American Psychological Association (APA) referencing style is more than a way of formatting citations. It has a number of distinctive features relating to layout, font and use of language. It is particularly popular in disciplines that adopt reflective processes in practice and in writing.

How to cite the reference in the text in the APA style

Plagiarism is not a new phenomenon nor is it one that is confined to academia (Fairfull & Hunter, 2009). In publishing, for example, several notorious cases of plagiarism exist where the text and plot of a best seller have close similarities to the text and plot of another book by another author (Scribner, 2006). However, it is not only with the printed word that plagiarism can take place. Cruikshanks (2012) suggests that plagiarism occurs when a junior member of staff originates an idea that a senior member then portrays as their own without any acknowledgement of the true originator of the idea. As Peel (1944) asserts, the practice of using someone else's intellectual property without attributing it to the author of that text, idea or image amounts to theft. Nevertheless, in academia, our students have great difficulty with this concept, in part, because they often do not know that plagiarism comes in many different guises – some estimates identify 20 variations (Schneider *et al.*, 2010). We give the broad instruction that students should use their own words because, in many cases, they lack the skills of summarising and paraphrasing that would enable them to avoid committing plagiarism (Ross, 2003). However, Williams (as cited in Douglas, 2010) viewed the whole issue of plagiarism as raising a more fundamental issue, and that is related to critical thinking. As Ivor Scott, a well-published academic author frequently cited in academic articles and other texts notes

If imitation is the sincerest form of flattery, then finding my words coming back at me verbatim in my students' essays, should make me exceedingly flattered, but, in fact, makes me incredibly angry. I am not the ultimate authority in my field and I would like to have my words, thoughts and ideas challenged, not copied.

Scott, 2011, p. 55

Thus, it is vital that students understand exactly what comprises plagiarism – in all its forms. For academia, there is a duty to ensure that students are trained in the skills of citation, referencing, summarising and paraphrasing at an early stage in their studies. This will mean that they can use the work of others in a responsible way to support their line of reasoning and demonstrate "the skills of critical thinking that distinguish university education" (Chatsworth, 2005, p. 34).

How to lay out the Reference List in the APA Style

References

Chatsworth, B. (2005). Academic education. In M. Diddle (Ed.), *Making the student mind* (2nd ed., pp. 103–115). Edinburgh: Norloch Publishing.

Cruikshanks, R. (2012). *Working the system* [online]. Retrieved from http://www.hvn.ac.uk/truth/trickco.htm.

Douglas, G. (2010). *Reasoning critically: The ethical way.* Richmond: Swaledale Press.

Fairfull, B. & Hunter, A. (2009). *Division of labour: The ethical impact.* London: Thames Press.

Peel, R. (1944). *Wealth by stealth.* Melbourne: Outback Press.

Ross, F. (2003). *The power of the pen.* Dover: Kentish Press.

Schneider, F., Kleister, C., Krebs, M. & Schnecke, V. (2010). *Word for word.* Düsseldorf, Rhein Verlag.

Scott, I. (Ed.). (2011). *The reality of learning.* Inverness: Heatherbank Press.

Scribner, A. (2006). Authorship by proxy: the case of the non-original best-seller. *Journal of Professional Ethics, 2*(3), 51–59.

Note: APA spacing for the reference list should be double-line. Space limitations within this publication make it difficult to emulate this exactly.

Quotations in the text following the APA Style

Long quotes: in APA, the indented style (five spaces from margin) shown in the sample text is only applied for quotations greater than 40 words.

Short quotes: layout is shown below.

> The movement of words within a sentence or the substitution of a synonym is not sufficient to avoid plagiarism and it is certainly not what could be regarded as "a summary of the key idea of the text". (Chatsworth, 2005, p. 19)
>
> According to Douglas (2010), "stealing another person's ideas is tantamount to stealing their soul" (p. 82).

Specific features

This citation style is complex because it is prescriptive on a variety of issues and involves highly detailed instructions. These dictate: font, typeface, spacing, pagination, layout and presentation. Use of active voice and personal pronouns are indicated. The style requires a framework that should follow: Title page, Abstract, Body of text, References, Appendixes, Footnotes, Tables, Figure captions, Figures. Detailed formats apply in APA for each of these sections. The points below cover some of the more basic stipulations.

In text:

- Margin of one inch (2.5 cm) top, bottom and both sides.
- Font should be Times New Roman, 12 pt. and double-lined spacing.
- Pages should be numbered and positioned 1" (2.5 cm) from right edge of paper and first line of pages; first few words of title of paper should be positioned at top of each page five character spaces to the left of the page number. This is not required in the Figures section.
- Use of personal pronouns (I/we) expected; active voice preferred to passive.
- Books with two authors cited: both names used at all times; the ampersand (&) should be used rather than the word 'and'.
- Book with 3+ authors, all authors are included at first mention and thereafter, the first author's name followed by et al. (no italics) is used.

Reference list:

- Arrange in alphabetical order by the first letter of the surname of the first author.

- Margins should be left-justified; first line of reference on left margin with subsequent lines indented by five character spaces; no justification on right edge.

- Reference list should be double-spaced; left justified for first line; subsequent lines should be indented five character spaces.

- If no date is given for an electronic reference, then use the abbreviation **n.d.** which stands for 'no date'. This applies to the reference list and the in-text citation.

- Italicise titles of books and journals; italicise periodical volume numbers.

- Where one author has more than one publication, order them by publication date, from oldest to newest.

- For US publications, the location should be given as city and state with two-letter postal abbreviation (e.g. Richmond, VA).

Further information available from: American Psychological Association (2010). *Publication Manual of the American Psychological Association* (5th ed.). Washington, DC: American Psychological Association. A useful online tutorial is available at *www.apa.org*.

How to list different types of source in the APA Style

Hard copy resources	
Book by one author	Ross, F. (2003). *The power of the pen.* Dover: Kentish Press.
Book by two authors	Fairfull, B. & Hunter, A. (2009). *Division of labour: The ethical impact.* London: Thames Press.
Book with three or more authors	Schneider, F., Kleister, C., Krebs, M. & Schnecke, V. (2010). *Word for word.* Düsseldorf: Rhein Verlag.
Edition of book other than the first	Dixon, R. (2009). *Writing for meaning* (3rd ed.). Perth, UK: Priority Publications.
Book under editorship	Scott, I. (Ed.). (2011). *The reality of learning.* Inverness: Heatherbank Press.
Chapter in an edited book	Chatsworth, B. (2005). Academic education. In M. Diddle (Ed.), *Making the student mind* (pp. 52–9). Edinburgh: Norloch Publishing.

Hard copy resources	
Secondary referencing – where the original text is not available and the reference relates to a citation in a text which you have read (see **Ch 7**).	Douglas, G. (2010). *Reasoning critically: The ethical way.* Richmond: Swaledale Press. (The book cited was Williams, but the book *read* by the writer of the essay was Douglas (2010) which is the one to list in the Reference List.)
Journal article	Scribner, A. (2006). Authorship by proxy: the case of the non-original best-seller. *Journal of Professional Ethics,* 2(3), 51–59. Note that pp. (for pages) is not included in cases of journal referencing.
Newspaper article	Todd, C. (2011, July 22). All the evidence shows writing is in decline. *Taymouth Times,* pp. 15. Note for newspapers the abbreviation p. or pp. is included; columns are indicated by page number followed by A or B.
Newspaper article no author	Speaking for yourself – citation without plagiarism. (2009, August 1). *The Writers' Courier,* p. 5.

Online resources
URLs can potentially change and material can become unobtainable. A system of using the Digital Object Indentifier (DOI) has been introduced to avoid this problem. It gives stability and longevity to the material should a URL 'die'. Some online documents may be referenced using their unique DOI. DOIs are alphanumeric and will look similar to this format: doi:0000000/000000000000. For DOI information: http://www.crossref.org/guestquery. APA Style favours the use of DOIs.

Internet references including e-books	Cruikshanks, R. (2012). *Working the system* [online]. Retrieved from: http://www.hvn.ac.uk/truth/trickco.htm.
Online journal article with DOI	Kay, J. (2008). Plagiarism detection: good use of academic time. *Journal of the New Age, 35,* 134–140. doi:10.11111/123456782008.
Internet references: e-journals (URL)	Ross, F. (2010). Coping with academic 'dementia'. *Ethical Medical Research* [online], 5(14). Retrieved from: http://ethmed.ac.ic/archive000002010/mis.htm
Online newspaper	Saunders, S. (2009, July 14). University plagiarism tracking devices. *Tayside Morning Chronicle.* Retrieved from: http://www.dundeenews.org/plagiarism-tracking-devices.1234567.html.
Film, video, television or radio programme	Dangerfield, S. (Producer and Director) (2010). The Wordmeister. [Film] Bonn: Deutschefernsehen.

Continued overleaf

Online resources	
Weblog (BLOG)	M. Stuart. (2009, May 8). Truth and nothing but the truth: fact and opinion in citation. [Web log comment.] Retrieved from: http://www. margaretstewart.com/blog.
Wiki	Sharing the blame: plagiarism and group projects. Retrieved April 1 2009, from School Forum wiki: http://wiki.schoolforum/plagiarism.com/ sharing+and+the+blame. Since Wiki content is usually generated by multiple users, usually no author is named. Wikis are not refereed and content cannot be guaranteed.
Website	If this is a general website and it is cited within the text, then it is not necessary to include it in the Reference List. For example: The art of summarising and paraphrasing is not a dying one, but it could do with the kiss of life (http://www.languageofscience.com).
Website with named author	For extensive web pages, give URL for home page. Smith and Murray (2011, December 1). Retrieved from: http://www.effectiveeditor.com.
Unknown date	If there is no date on web page, the abbreviation n.d. (no date) should be used. Developing writing and provenance of text. n.d. British Authors for Justice, London. http:// wwwBAJ.co.uk/britishauthors.htm.
Email communication	Emails are not listed in the references, but can be inserted in round brackets in the text: (A. Yorke, personal communication, August 26, 2010).

CHICAGO STYLE

This referencing style is a footnote form of referencing that enables the reader to see the full bibliographic details on the first page that the reference is made. Subsequent references of the same source do not give this level of detail. A full listing of the bibliographical details is given at the end of the work. (See Ch 10.) There are two options for layout and presentation; these are outlined below.

How to cite the reference in the text in the Chicago Style

[Note that the Chicago Manual stipulates a double-line spacing layout. For reasons of space 1.5 line spacing is used in this model. Normally, everything from title to bibliography should be in double-line spacing.]

Plagiarism is not a new phenomenon nor is it one that is confined to academia.[1] In publishing, for example, there are several notorious cases where a best seller has been shown to be closely similar to another book by another author.[2] However, it is not only with the printed word that plagiarism can take place. Cruikshanks[3] suggests that plagiarism occurs when an idea originated by a junior member of staff is plagiarised by a senior member who portrays it as their own without any acknowledgement of the true originator of the idea. As Peel[4] asserts, the practice of using someone else's intellectual property without attributing it to the author of that text, idea or image amounts to theft. Nevertheless, in academia, students have great difficulty with this concept, in part, because they often do not know that plagiarism comes in many different guises – some estimates identify 20 variations.[5] The broad instruction that students should use their own words is often unhelpful because, in many cases, as noted by Ross[6], they lack the skills of summarising and paraphrasing that would enable them to avoid committing plagiarism. However, Williams[7] has contended that the whole issue of plagiarism raises a more fundamental issue and that is related to critical thinking. As Ivor Scott [8], a well-published academic author frequently cited in academic articles and other texts notes

If imitation is the sincerest form of flattery, then finding my words coming back at me verbatim in my students' essays, should make me exceedingly flattered, but, in fact, makes me incredibly angry. I am not the ultimate authority in my field and I would like to have my words, thoughts and ideas challenged, not copied.

Thus, it is vital that students understand exactly what comprises plagiarism – in all its forms.[9] For academia, there is a duty to ensure that students are trained in the skills of citation, referencing, summarising and paraphrasing at an early stage in their studies.[10] This will mean that they can use the work of others in a responsible way to support their line of reasoning and demonstrate "the skills of critical thinking that distinguish university education".[11]

How to lay out the Footnotes and the Reference List (Bibliography) in the Chicago Style

There are two options:

1 Footnotes are at the bottom of the page beneath a line across the page or as a list of endnotes at the end of the text (as below) with a full bibliography of all works cited at the end of the text.

2 Full citations in the footnotes or endnotes for the first mention and thereafter as concise notes (See **Ch 10**); there is no bibliography.

Footnotes

1.   B. Fairfull and A. Hunter, *Division of Labour: the Ethical Impact* (London:Thames Press, 2009), 101.

2.   A. Scribner, "Authorship by Proxy: the Case of the Non-original Best-seller," *Journal of Professional Ethics*, 15, no. 3 (2006): 59.

3.   R. Cruikshanks, "Working the Style," *Online Journal of Ethics and Standards* 15 no.1 (2012); available from http://www.hvn.ac.uk/truth/trickco.htm. Internet. Accessed 18 March 2012.

4.   R. Peel, *Wealth by Stealth* (Melbourne: Outback Press, 1944), 89.

5.   F. Schneider et al., *Word for Word* (Düsseldorf: Rhein Verlag, 2010), 22.

6.   F. Ross, *The Power of the Pen* (Dover: Kentish Press, 2003), 156.

7.   G. Douglas, *Reasoning Critically: The Ethical Way* (Richmond: Swaledale Press, 2010), 72.

8.   I. Scott ed. *The Reality of Learning* (Inverness: Heatherbank Press, 2011), 4.

9.   ibid. 10.

10.   B. Chatsworth, "Academic Education" in *Making the Student Mind*, ed. M. Diddle (Edinburgh: Norloch Publishing, 2005),109.

11.   Douglas, op.cit. p. 77.

Bibliography

Chatsworth, B. "Academic Education." In: *Making the Student Mind*, edited by M. Diddle, 103–115. Edinburgh: Norloch Publishing, 2005.

Cruikshanks, R. "Working the Style." *Online Journal of Ethics and Standards* 15 no.1 (2005): 24–32. Accessed October 18, 2011. http://www.hvn.ac.uk/truth/trickco.htm.

Douglas, G. *Reasoning Critically: the Ethical Way*. Richmond: Swaledale Press, 2010.

Fairfull, B. and A. Hunter. *Division of Labour: the Ethical Impact*. London: Thames Press, 2009.

Peel, R. *Wealth by Stealth*. Melbourne: Outback Press, 1944.

Ross, F. *The Power of the Pen*. Dover: Kentish Press, 2003.

Schneider, F. C. Kleister, M. Krebs, and V. Schnecke. *Word for Word*. Düsseldorf: Rhein Verlag, 2010.

Scott, I. ed. *The Reality of Learning*. Inverness: Heatherbank Press, 2011.

Scribner, A. "Authorship by Proxy: the Case of the Non-original Best-seller," *Journal of Professional Ethics* 15, no. 3 (2006): 59.

Quotations in the text following the Chicago Style

Short quotations

The movement of words within a sentence or the substitution of a synonym is not sufficient to avoid plagiarism and it is certainly not what could be regarded as "a summary of the key idea of the text".[7]

According to Douglas[4], "stealing another person's ideas is tantamount to stealing their soul".

If you need to make **a quote within a quote**, then there are two interpretations: British and US American. In the British convention, the long quotation is in single quotation marks and the quotation within that quote is in double quotation marks.

British English version:

The review noted that 'head teachers are taking early retirement as they would rather go on "gardening leave" than face the bureaucracy of constant inspections'.

American English version:

The review noted that "head teachers are taking early retirement as they would rather go on 'gardening leave' than face the bureaucracy of constant inspections".

Long quotations

If the quotation is more than four manuscript lines, then the text of the quotation should be indented by one or two tab spaces from the left-hand margin and amend to single line spacing for that quotation alone.

It has been found that children in schools are often

> ... found to be lacking those skills of knowing how to put the ideas of others into their own words without using the source text verbatim. In an age where text messaging invites modifications of language that abbreviate whole words to a single letter or figure, it appears that this skill in brevity has not translated into adequate styles of paraphrasing abstract concepts within academic contexts. [8]

Specific features

Abbreviations:

- *ibid.* means in the same place as the immediately preceding citation (sometimes with a different page number) (see also **Ch 10**);
- *op. cit.* means in the previously cited work by the same author (sometimes with different page number) (see also **Ch 10**); and
- *et al.* which means 'and others' and is used in the Chicago style to indicate the authorship when four or more authors have contributed to the work. The term *et al.* can be used in the footnotes/endnotes but not in the final bibliographical reference list where the names of all authors should be given (see also **Ch 10**).

Layout:

- citation numbers in text should be in superscript position;
- in footnotes/endnotes, indent first line by 1.25cm (run-on lines begin at margin). Use standard size figures followed by a full stop and two character spaces before typing the bibliographical information;
- **on the bibliographical list**, entries are single-spaced with double-spacing between entries;
    - the first line of entry should be positioned at the left margin;
    - any follow-on lines for the same entry should begin five character spaces in from the left margin;
    - where one author has been cited in two or more publications, then use three dashes to replace the author's name in all entries after the first.

Bibliography in the Chicago Style (16th edition, 2010)

There are two options:

1 Footnotes *or* endnotes with a full bibliography of all resources cited in the notes.

2 Full citations/endnotes on the first time of citing, thereafter in simplified forms (see **Ch 10**). No bibliography.

Hard copy resources	Position	Example
Book by one author	In footnote/ endnote	1. F. Graham, *Ethical Dilemmas in Academia*. (Perth: Fair City Press, 2007), 106. (final item is page number for citation)
	In reference list	Graham, F. *Ethical Dilemmas in Academia*. Perth: Fair City Press, 2007.
Book by two authors	In footnote/ endnote	2. B, Fairfull and A. Hunter, *Division of Labour: the Ethical Impact*. (London: Thames Press; 2009), 22.
	In reference list	Fairfull B., and A. Hunter. *Division of Labour: the Ethical Impact*. London: Thames Press, 2009.
Book with four or more authors	In footnote/ endnote	For four or more authors: in text First Author et al.; list all in the bibliography. 3. Schneider, F.J. et al., *Word for Word*. (Düsseldorf: Rhein Verlag, 2010), 60.
	In reference list	Schneider, F.J., C.K. Kleister, M, Krebs, and V. Schnecke. *Word for Word*. Düsseldorf: Rhein Verlag, 2010, 55–62.
Book under editorship	In footnote/ endnote	4. I. Scott, ed. *The Reality of Learning*. (Inverness: Heatherbank Press, 2011), 34.
	In reference list	Scott, I. (editor) *The Reality of Learning*. Inverness: Heatherbank Press, 2011.
Chapter in a book	In footnote/ endnote	5. B. Chatsworth, "Academic Education," in *Making the Student Mind*, ed. M. Diddle (Edinburgh: Norloch Publishing, 2005), 109.
	In reference list	Chatsworth, B. "*Academic Education.*" In Making the Student Mind, edited by M. Diddle, 103–115, Edinburgh: Norloch Publishing, 2005.

Continued overleaf

Hard copy resources	Position	Example
Secondary referencing (see **Ch 7**). This is discouraged in Chicago Style.	In footnote/ endnote	6. Werner Williams, "*Beyond the Ethical Pale*" (Berlin: Deutscher Press, 1996), 72, quoted in Graham Douglas, *Reasoning critically: the ethical way* (Richmond: Swaledale Press, 2010), 93.
	In reference list	Include both sources: Douglas, G. 2010. *Reasoning critically: the ethical way.* Richmond: Swaledale Press, 2010. Williams, W. 1996. *Beyond the ethical pale.* Berlin: Deutscher Press: 309, quoted in Douglas, G. *Reasoning critically: the ethical way* (2010), 93.
Journal article	In footnote/ endnote	7. A. Scribner, "Authorship by Proxy: the Case of the Non-original Best-seller," *Journal of Professional Ethics* 33, no. 4 (2006): 56.
	In reference list	Scribner, A. "Authorship by Proxy: the Case of the Non-original Best-seller." *Journal of Professional Ethics* 33, no. 4 (2006): 51–9.
Newspaper article	In footnote/ endnote	Newspaper articles not usually included in reference list/bibliography. Can be cited within the text. e.g. As Angus Swankie reported in a Taymouth Times article on July 22, 2008, … If cited in a note, the format would be: 8. Angus Swankie, "All the Evidence Shows." *Taymouth Times.* 22 July 2008, 15.
	In reference list	Not routinely included in this listing.

Online resources

URLs can potentially change and material can become unobtainable. A system of using the Digital Object Identifier (DOI) has been introduced to avoid this problem. It will give stability and longevity to the material should a URL 'die'. Some online documents may be referenced using their unique DOI. DOIs are alphanumeric. DOIs look similar to this format: doi:0000000/000000000000. Where no DOI is available, give the URL.

Internet references including e-books	In footnote/ endnote	9. Margaret Douglas, *The Dialogue of Citation: Building the Argument* (Glasgow: Clyde Press, 2006), accessed March 31, 2011, http://www.ethicalenquiries.com/content/lindsay/192445.html.
	In reference list	Douglas, Margaret. *The Dialogue of Citation: Building the Argument.* Glasgow: Clyde Press, 2006. Accessed March 31, 2011. http://www.ethicalenquiries.com/content/lindsay/192445.html.

Online resources

e-journals	In footnote/endnote	**With URL:**
		10. Frances Ross, 2010, "Coping with academic 'dementia' in the work place," *Ethical Medical Research*, 5 (2010): 114–130, accessed January 11, 2011, http://ethmed.ac.ic/archive000002010/mis.htm
		Or with DOI:
		11. Frances Ross, 2010, "Coping with academic 'dementia' in the work place," *Ethical Medical Research*, 5 (2010): 114–130, accessed January 11, 2011, doi:10.1066/292822
	In reference list	Ross, F. "Coping with academic 'dementia' in the work place." *Ethical Medical Research*. 5 (2010): 114–130. Accessed January 11, 2011. doi:10.1066/292822
Journal article online	In footnote/endnote	12. R. Cruikshanks, "Working the Style," *Online Journal of Ethics and Standards* 15 no.1 (2005): 24–32, accessed October 18, 2011: http://www.hvn.ac.uk/truth/tricko.htm
	In reference list	Cruikshanks, R. "Working the Style," *Online Journal of Ethics and Standards* 15 no. 1 (2005): 24–32. Accessed October 18, 2011. http://www.hvn.ac.uk/truth/tricko.htm.
Online newspaper	In footnote/endnote	13. Stanley Saunders, "University plagiarism tracking devices," *Tayside Morning Chronicle,* July 21 2009, 35, accessed October 18, 2010. www.dundeenews.org/plagiarism-tracking-devices.1234567.html.
	In reference list	Not listed in bibliography/reference list.
Newspaper article without a named author	In footnote/endnote	14. "Speaking for yourself – citation without plagiarism," *The Writers' Courier,* April 30, 2010, 5, accessed August 31, 2011. http://writerscourier.com/2010/08/citation_plagiarism.html
	In reference list	Not listed in bibliography/reference list.
Film, video, television or radio programme	In footnote/endnote	15. The Wordmeister, film, directed by Stanley Dangerfield (2010) [Bonn, DFS]. Video
	In reference list	The Wordmeister. Produced and directed by Stanley Dangerfield. Bonn: DFS, 2010.

Continued overleaf

Online resources

Weblog (BLOG)	In footnote/endnote	Usually omitted from bibliography/reference list. Can be cited within text e.g. In a comment posted to Badersblog on May 8, 2010, ... or this can be cited in a footnote: 16. Megan, May 8, 2009 (3.30 a.m.), comment on Bernhardt Bader, "Truth and nothing but the truth: fact and opinion in citation," Badersblog, May 7,2009.
	In reference list	Not listed in bibliography/reference list.
Wiki	In footnote/endnote	Since wiki content is usually generated by multiple users, usually no author is named. The entry in the text might be: 17. Plagiarism wiki (2009) offers an explanation that ... or (Plagiarism wiki 2009).
	In reference list	Plagiarism wiki 2009, "Sharing the blame: plagiarism and group projects", wiki article, April 1, viewed April 28, 2009, http://plagiarism.pbwikie.com/sharing+and+the+blame.
Website	In footnote/endnote	Websites are usually cited within the text, for example: 'In the run-up to the Olympics, information will be posted on its website ...' If you are required to cite a website, the format is as follows: "Olympic Frenzy for Tickets," modified, March 31, 2012, http://www.olympus2012/tickets/allocation.html.
	In reference list	Not listed in bibliography/reference list.
Email communication or text message	In footnote/endnote	Emails and text messages can be cited within the text. This is in preference to a note and they are not listed in the bibliography. In an email message to the author on April 1, 2012, Alan Yorke commented that ...
	In reference list	Not listed in bibliography/reference list.

HARVARD STYLE

This referencing style has the advantage of being simpler, quicker and possibly more readily adjustable than some other styles. It is used internationally in a wide range of fields and provides author/date information in the text. Note that there are various interpretations of the style. This example follows BS5605:1990.

How to cite the reference in the text in Harvard Style

Plagiarism is not a new phenomenon nor is it one that is confined to academia (Fairfull and Hunter, 2009). In publishing, for example, there are several notorious cases where a best seller has been shown to be closely similar to another book by another author (Scribner, 2006). However, it is not only with the printed word that plagiarism can take place. Cruikshanks (2012) suggested that plagiarism occurs when an idea originated by a junior member of staff is plagiarised by a senior member who portrays it as their own without any acknowledgement of the true originator of the idea. As Peel (1944) asserted, the practice of using someone else's intellectual property without attributing it to the author of that text, idea or image amounts to theft. Nevertheless, in academia, students have great difficulty with this concept, in part, because they often do not know that plagiarism comes in many different guises – some estimates identify 20 variations (Schneider *et al.*, 2010). The broad instruction that students should use their own words is often unhelpful because, in many cases, as noted by Ross (2003), they lack the skills of summarising and paraphrasing that would enable them to avoid committing plagiarism. However, the whole issue of plagiarism raises a more fundamental issue and that is related to critical thinking (Williams, 1996 cited in Douglas, 2011). As, Ivor Scott, a well-published academic author frequently cited in academic articles and other texts noted

> If imitation is the sincerest form of flattery, then finding my words coming back at me verbatim in my students' essays, should make me exceedingly flattered, but, in fact, makes me incredibly angry. I am not the ultimate authority in my field and I would like to have my words, thoughts and ideas challenged, not copied.
>
> (Scott, 2011, p. 55)

Thus, it is vital that students understand exactly what comprises plagiarism – in all its forms. For academia, there is a duty to ensure that students are trained in the skills of citation, referencing, summarising and paraphrasing at an early stage in their studies. This will mean that they can use the work of others in a responsible way to support their line of reasoning and demonstrate 'the skills of critical thinking that distinguish university education' (Chatsworth, 2005).

How to lay out the Reference List in Harvard Style

Reference List

Chatsworth, B., 2005. Academic education. In: M. Diddle, ed. *Making the student mind.* Edinburgh: Norloch Publishing, 103–115.

Cruikshanks, R., 2012. *Working the system* [online]. York: Shambles Press: Available at: http://www.hvn.ac.uk/truth/trickco.htm [Accessed 4 April 2012].

Douglas, G., 2000. *Reasoning critically: the ethical way.* Richmond: Swaledale Press.

Fairfull, B. and Hunter, A., 2009. *Division of labour: the ethical impact.* London: Thames Press.

Taymouth Times. 2008. All the evidence shows …. *Taymouth Times*, July 22, p.15.

Peel, R., 1944. *Wealth by stealth.* Melbourne: Outback Press.

Ross, F., 2003. *The power of the pen.* Dover: Kentish Press.

Schneider, F., Kleister, C., Krebs, M. and Schnecke, V., 2010. *Word for word.* Düsseldorf: Rhein Verlag.

Scott, I., ed., 2011. *The reality of learning.* Inverness: Heatherbank Press.

Scribner, A., 2006. Authorship by proxy: the case of the non-original best-seller. *Journal of Professional Ethics* 2(3), 51–59.

Citations in the text following the Harvard Style

In this text, the two principal modes of citation in text are used. These are:

1. **Information prominent,** where the information about the author is of secondary importance relative to the idea that is being reported. In the text opposite, the following authors are cited using the information prominent style, that is, where the author's name is given at the end of the sentence in which reference to that person's work has been made.

   e.g. (Fairfull and Hunter, 2009)

Plagiarism is not a new phenomenon nor is it one that is confined to academia (Fairfull and Hunter, 2009).

Family name of author, comma plus date of publication ALL inside round brackets

---

2. **Author prominent**, where the role of the author as a key player in the debate or research field is shown by incorporating the author's family name and the date of the publication within the sentence.

   e.g. Cruikshanks (2012)

```
┌─────────────────────┐   ┌─────────────────────┐
│ Family name of author│   │ Date only in brackets│
└─────────────────────┘   └─────────────────────┘
          \                  /
           \                /
```

Cruikshanks (2012) **suggested** that plagiarism occurs when an idea originated by a junior member of staff is plagiarised by a senior member who portrays it as their own without any acknowledgement of the true originator of the idea.

Specific features

Abbreviations

et al. means 'and others'. It is usually used when citing **in the text** where there are more than two authors involved in the compilation of the book. Therefore, in the model text, it can be seen that the expression 'Schneider *et al.*', is used. Note that **in the reference list**, all the authors are listed (family name and initial of first name).

Quotations in the text following the Harvard Style

Long quotes (40+ words) should be indented in the text. The layout is illustrated in the long quote (Scott, 2011) in the text on page 143. Note: single line spacing and no quotation marks.

Short quotes (fewer than 40 words) are integrated in a sentence and placed within single quotation marks, for example:

According to Douglas (2000) 'stealing another person's ideas is tantamount to stealing their soul' (p. 82).

Presentation notes

- Arrange references on list in alphabetical order by the first letter of the surname of the first author.
- Leave double space between each entry.
- In this version of the Harvard Style, only the first words of book titles are capitalised. Except for proper nouns (names of people, places and organisations), all other words are in lower case.
- If you need to cite two (or more) pieces of work published within

the same year by the same author, then the convention is to refer to these texts as 2005a, 2005b and so on.

- In some interpretations of this method the first line of every entry is indented five character spaces from the left margin. Our view is that this creates an untidy page where it is difficult to identify the author quickly.

Additional Harvard facts

- The Harvard Style does not require the recording of the ISBN number which is a detail required by booksellers but is not routinely the reference used for cataloguing books in an academic library such as those found in universities.

- The Harvard Style has the advantage over other styles in that it is necessary to record all the bibliographical details only once in the reference list rather than multiple times as in some other styles.

How to list different types of source following the Harvard Style

Hard copy resources	Basic format: Author surname|author initial|date|title|place of publication|publisher
Book by one author	Ross, F., 2003. *The power of the pen.* Dover: Kentish Press.
Book by two authors	Fairfull, B. and Hunter, A., 2009. *Division of labour: the ethical impact.* London: Thames Press.
Book with three or more authors	Schneider, F., Kleister, C., Krebs, M. and Schnecke, V., 2001. *Word for word.* Düsseldorf: Rhein Verlag.
Book under editorship	Scott, I., ed., 2011. *The reality of learning.* Inverness: Heatherbank Press.
Chapter in a book	Chatsworth, B., 2005. Academic education. In: M. Diddle, ed. *Making the student mind.* Edinburgh: Norloch Publishing, 103–115.
Secondary referencing – where the original text is not available and the reference relates to a citation in a text which you have read (see **Ch 7**).	Douglas, G., 2010. *Reasoning critically: the ethical way.* Richmond: Swaledale Press. (In the sample text the book cited was Williams, 1996, but the book READ by the writer of the essay was Douglas 2010 which is the one to list in the reference list.)
Journal article	Scribner, A., 2006. Authorship by proxy: the case of the non-original best-seller. *Journal of Professional Ethics* 2(3), 51–59.
Newspaper article	*Taymouth Times.* 20011. All the evidence shows .... *Taymouth Times,* July 22nd, p. 15.

Online resources	
Internet references including e-books	Cruikshanks, R., 2012. *Working the system* [online]. York: Shambles Press. Available from: http://www.hvn.ac.uk/truth/trickco.htm. [Accessed 4 April 2012]
Internet references: e-journals	Ross, F., 2010. Coping with academic 'dementia'. *Ethical Medical Research* [online], 5(14). Available from: <http://ethmed.ac.ic/archive000002010/mis.htm> [Accessed 11 January 2011]
Journal article	Kay, J., 2008. Plagiarism detection: is it a good use of academic time? *Journal of the New Age*, 35(2), 134–140. Available at Academic Journals Database. [Accessed 11 April 2008].
Online newspaper	Saunders, S. 2009. University plagiarism tracking devices. *Tayside Morning Chronicle*, 14 July, p. 20. Available at: www.dundeenews.org/university-plagiarism-tracking-devices. 1234567.html
Newspaper article without a named author	'Speaking for yourself – citation without plagiarism', *The Writers' Courier*, 1st April 2000, p. 5. Available at: www.historynews.co.uk, [Accessed 1 August 2009].
Film, video, television or radio programme	Include the title, year of recording, format, publisher/distributor, place of recording, date of recording (if appropriate). The Wordmeister, 2008, television programme, Deutsch FS, Bonn, 12th August.
Weblog (BLOG)	Give the author name and the year of posting. Stuart, M. 2009, Truth and nothing but the truth: fact and opinion in citation, weblog, accessed 8th May 2009, http://www.margaretstewart.com/blog.
Wiki	Since wiki content is usually generated by multiple users, usually no author is named. 'Sharing the blame: plagiarism and group projects', wiki article, April 1, 2009, accessed 5 April 2009, http://plagiarism.pbwikie.com/sharing+and+the+blame.
Website	Include author name/person responsible for site, year (date of creation/update), name of sponsor of site, location of sponsor (if known), accessed (day, month, year), URL or internet address in pointed brackets < >. Try to ensure that the URL is given without a line-break interruption. Intercontinental Plagiarism Detection and Compliance Board 2010, New York, Available at: www.ipdcb.org. [Accessed 14 June 2011].
Unknown author of website	NB: cite only the page title and the date. *Stealing the idea or stealing the text*, 2009, Available at: http://www.effectiveeditor.com. [Accessed 1 December 2011].

Continued overleaf

Online resources	
Unknown date	If there is no date on web page, the abbreviation n.d. (no date) should be used. Developing writing and provenance of text, n.d., British Authors for Justice, London, Available at: http://www.BAJ.co.uk/britishauthors.htm. [Accessed 30 September 2011].
Email communication	Emails are regarded as 'personal communication' and are not normally used in the reference list so that they cannot be tracked to the source by the reader. However, if you are required to cite emails, then note that there is some modification in the way the email is presented i.e. with initial preceding surname. Yorke, A., 2010, email 26th August, A.Yorke@mailshot.com.

14

MODERN LANGUAGES ASSOCIATION (MLA) STYLE

This style is claimed to be one of the more popular modes of referencing used in the USA by disciplines in Arts and Humanities. It uses a style of giving author and page information in the text, but no date is included within the text. The sources are listed alphabetically in the list of references at the end of the work. Note the indentation layout convention in the Works Cited listing.

How to cite the reference in the text

Plagiarism is not a new phenomenon nor is it one that is confined to academia (Fairfull and Hunter 69). In publishing, for example, there are several notorious cases where a best seller has been shown to be closely similar to another book by another author (Scribner 35). However, it is not only with the printed word that plagiarism can take place. Cruikshanks suggests that plagiarism occurs when an idea originated by a junior member of staff is plagiarised by a senior member who portrays it as their own without any acknowledgement of the true originator of the idea (90). As Peel asserts, the practice of using someone else's intellectual property without attributing it to the author of that text, idea or image amounts to theft (50–1). Nevertheless, in academia, students have great difficulty with this concept, in part, because they often do not know that plagiarism comes in many different guises – some estimates identify 20 variations (Schneider *et al.* 67). The broad instruction that students should use their own words is often unhelpful because, in many cases, as noted by Ross, they lack the skills of summarising and paraphrasing that would enable them to avoid committing plagiarism (84). However, Williams has suggested that the whole issue of plagiarism raises a more fundamental issue and that is related to critical thinking (qtd. in Douglas 99–101). As, Ivor Scott, a well-published academic author frequently cited in academic articles and other texts notes

> If imitation is the sincerest form of flattery, then finding my words coming back at me verbatim in my students' essays, should make me exceedingly flattered, but, in fact, makes me incredibly angry. I am not the ultimate authority in my field and I would like to have my words, thoughts and ideas challenged, not copied. Scott 55

Thus, it is vital that students understand exactly what comprises plagiarism – in all its forms. For academia, there is a duty to ensure that students are trained in the skills of citation, referencing, summarising and paraphrasing at an early stage in their studies. This will mean that they can use the work of others in a responsible way to support their line of reasoning and demonstrate 'the skills of critical thinking that distinguish university education' (Chatsworth 45).

How to lay out the Work Cited following the MLA Style

Works cited

Chatsworth, B. 'Academic Education.' *Making the Student Mind*. M. Diddle, Edinburgh: Norloch Publishing, 2005: 103–115. Print.

Cruikshanks, R. '*Working the Style*.' 31 December 2012. 1 April 2005, e-book.

Douglas, G. *Reasoning Critically: the Ethical Way*. Richmond: Swaledale Press, 2010. Print.

Fairfull, B. and Hunter, A. *Division of Labour: the Ethical Impact*. London: Thames Press, 2009. Print.

Peel, R. *Wealth by Stealth*. Melbourne: Outback Press, 1944. Print.

Ross, F. *The Power of the Pen*. Dover: Kentish Press, 2003. Print.

Schneider, F., Kleister, C., Krebs, M. and Schnecke, V. *Word for Word*. Düsseldorf: Rhein Verlag, 2010. Print.

Scott, I. (ed.) *The Reality of Learning*. Inverness: Heatherbank Press, 2011. Print.

Scribner, A. "Authorship by Proxy: the case of the Non-original Best-seller." *Journal of Professional Ethics* 2(3) (2006): 51–59. Print.

Quotations in the text following the MLA Style

Use double-line spacing (note that for reasons of space, here only 1.5 line spacing has been used).

Short quotations

In MLA Style, a short quotation is judged by length to be fewer than four lines of prose or three lines of poetry. Full stops come *after* the brackets.

The movement of words within a sentence or the substitution of a synonym is not sufficient to avoid plagiarism and it is certainly not what could be regarded as "a summary of the key idea of the text" (Taymouth Times 31).

According to Douglas "stealing another person's ideas is tantamount to stealing their soul" (82).

If you need to make **a quote within a quote**, then there are two interpretations: British and US American. In the British convention, the long quotation is in single quotation marks and the quotation within that quote is in double quotation marks.

British English version:

> The review noted that 'head teachers are taking early retirement as they would rather go on "gardening leave" than face the bureaucracy of constant inspections.'

American English version:

> The review noted that "head teachers are taking early retirement as they would rather go on 'gardening leave' than face the bureaucracy of constant inspections."

Long quotations

Quotations that would normally take up more than four typed lines are regarded as long quotations in MLA style. Unlike some other styles, long quotations maintain double-line spacing throughout; they should be typed 1" or 2.5 cm in from the left margin as a piece of indented text without quotation marks. i.e. one inch from left margin and with double-line spacing.

> Watt marks the desolation of the plot through the initial description that brings the reader directly into the narrative:
>
>> The boy looked into the middle distance with the tears glistening on his eyelashes, yet he uttered no sound as testimony to his emotion. His rite of passage from childhood to manhood had taken place in that sad place marked only by the sound of the gulls sweeping and swooping heedlessly above him. He turned and trudged towards the road and whatever he might meet on it. He would not return. (Watt 3)

See also **Chapter 7** and **Chapter 10** for further information about features of quotation.

Special features

In-text citation. The author's name can be included in the sentence, but the page number(s) should be in round brackets (...) at the end of the sentence not in the text.

Terminology. In this style, the list of references contains only the items that are cited in your text. The term used in MLA Style is 'Works Cited';

rather than 'Reference List'. Be guided by the guidelines provided in your course handbook.

Layout in works cited listing. Lists should be arranged on a new page using double-line spacing. Successive lines for the same entry are indented by five character spaces. This is called a hanging indent. Authors should be listed in alphabetical order by the surname of the first author; invert the surname and initial(s) of the first author and list subsequent authors of the same resource in initial(s)/first name then surname order. If you cite the same author more than once, use three hyphens instead of the author name in subsequent entries.

Use of italics. In some interpretations of this style, italics have replaced underlining of the titles of books, articles and chapters. The convention of underlining relates to the limitations of manual typewriters; word processors have enabled the use of italics rather than underlining. Since underlining can also be used in URLs, italicisation avoids confusion. Check your module guidelines on this or look at examples within your own discipline.

Use of capital letters. Titles should have capitals for the first word and each significant word, namely, nouns, pronouns, verbs, adjectives, adverbs; do not capitalise articles, short prepositions or conjunctions (except where these are the first word of a title. See Appendix 1 in this book for more information about these grammar terms.

URLs. MLA Style has discontinued use of URLs in citations for electronic resources.

Inverted commas. Put double inverted commas (quotation marks) around titles of journal articles, magazines and newspapers as well as titles of short stories, book chapters, poems and songs.

How to list different types of source following the MLA Style

Hard copy resources	Where relevant, page numbers are given at the end of the entry.
Book by one author	Douglas, G. *Reasoning Critically: the Ethical Way.* Richmond: Swaledale Press, 2010. Print.
Book by two authors	Fairfull, B. and A. Hunter. *Division of Labour: the Ethical Impact.* London: Thames Press, 2009. Print.

Hard copy resources	Where relevant, page numbers are given at the end of the entry.
Book with 3 or more authors OPTION 1	Schneider, F., C. Kleister, M. Krebs and V. Schnecke, *Word for Word*. Düsseldorf: Rhein Verlag, 2010. Print.
Book with three or more authors OPTION 2	Schneider, F., et al., *Word for Word*. Düsseldorf: Rhein Verlag, 2010. Print.
Book under editorship	Scott, I. ed. The Reality of Learning. Inverness: Heatherbank Press, 2011. Print.
Anthology or collection	Henderson, J., ed. *The Economics of Literature*. Dublin: Harp Press, 2010. Print.
Essay in a collection	Spark, L. "Talking in tongues." *Accessing Resources for Different Writing Styles*. Ed. M. Dyce. Cardiff: Owen Publications, 2009: 56–73. Print.
Secondary referencing	MLA recommendation is to locate the original source wherever possible. Where this is impossible, cite the original source in the text and the secondary source (the one that you did read) followed by the page number in brackets. Use 'qted. in' for 'quoted in'. In text: However, Williams has suggested that the whole issue of plagiarism raises a more fundamental issue and that is related to critical thinking (qtd. in Douglas 99). In references (only the source you read): Douglas, G. *Reasoning critically: the ethical way*. Richmond: Swaledale Press, 2010. Print.
Chapter in a book	Chatsworth, B. "Academic Education." *Making the Student Mind*. Ed. Mary Diddle, Edinburgh: Norloch Publishing, 2005: 103–115. Print.
Journal article	Scribner, A. "Authorship by Proxy: the Case of the Non-original Best-seller." *Journal of Professional Ethics* 2(3) (2006): 51–59. Print.
Newspaper article	"All the Evidence Shows." *Taymouth Times* 22 July 2011: 15. Print.
Online resources	**Date of publication is followed by organisation of sponsor of website, then date of access.**
Internet references including e-books	Cruikshanks, R. *Working the Style*. Haven University 3 Jun. 2011. 4 Apr. 2012. Web.
Internet references: e-journals n.p = no publisher	Ross, F. "Coping with Academic 'dementia' in the Workplace." *Ethical Medical Research*. 22 Feb. 2012. [online only journal] 5.14 (2011) n.p. Web.
Journal article in print and online	Kay, J. "Plagiarism detection: is it a good use of academic time?" *Journal of the New Age* 35.3 (2008): 134–140. Web. 28 April 2010.

Continued overleaf

Online resources	Date of publication is followed by organisation of sponsor of website, then date of access.
Online newspaper	Saunders, S. "University plagiarism tracking devices." *Tayside Morning Chronicle* 14 Jul. 2009. Web. 21 Jul. 2009.
Newspaper article without a named author	"Speaking for yourself – citation without plagiarism." *The Writers' Courier* 9 April 2010. Web. 30 Apr. 2010.
Film, video, television or radio programme	Film: Include the *Title*. Director. Performer. Film company. Year. *The Wordmeister.* Dir.Charles Gall. Perf. Ian Brown, Johan Black, Thomas Green, Antony Gray and Donna White. Deutsch FS. 2010. DVD. Television or radio programme: "Finding the Right Word." *Wordmeister Series.* Bremen. 20 Aug. 2011. Television.
Web discussion forum	Give the author name, title of posting in quotation marks and date of posting. Stuart, M. "Truth and Nothing but the Truth." Online posting. 8 May 2009. <http://www2.phil.com/forums/index.cfm?ABApp=88&Message_ID=12345>.
Wiki	Since wiki content is usually generated by multiple users, usually no author is named. "Anti-plagiarism." Wikisolutions, The Complete Guide to Avoiding Plagiarism. Wikisolutions Foundation. 5 Apr. 2009. Web. 18 October 2011. <http://wikisolutions.org/antiplagiarism>.
Website	*IPDCB Online.*14 Jun. 2010. Intercontinental Plagiarism Detection and Compliance Board 22 Oct. 2011. <www.ipdcb.org>.
Email communication	Yorke, A. "Re: Grammar Corrections." Email to the author, 26 Aug. 2010.
Tweets	Author's name and or user name (in brackets); entire Tweet (up to 140 characters) in inverted commas without changing capitalisation; date and time of message; form of message. Dunne, Martin (Reallydone). "Concrete stability in bridge struts questionable so propose suspension of work until damage potential assessed hopefully by 2PM." 1 April 2012, 9.34 a.m. Tweet.

15

VANCOUVER STYLE

This referencing style is commonly used in medical and scientific journals as well as in some of the humanities. The rules outlined in this chapter follow those set by the International Committee of Medical Journal Editors. The style is also known as Uniform Requirements for Manuscripts Submitted to Biomedical Journals. The *British Medical Journal* (*BMJ*) follows this style but with some minor adjustments (see www.bmj.com). It uses a numeric style where numbers are printed in the text within brackets like this (9) and relate to the corresponding number in the reference list at the end of the work.

How to cite the reference in the text

Plagiarism is not a new phenomenon nor is it one that is confined to academia. (1) In publishing, for example, there are several notorious cases where a best seller has been shown to be closely similar to another book by another author. (2) However, it is not only with the printed word that plagiarism can take place. Cruikshanks (3) suggests that plagiarism occurs when an idea originated by a junior member of staff is plagiarised by a senior member who portrays it as their own without any acknowledgement of the true originator of the idea. As Peel (4) asserts, the practice of using someone else's intellectual property without attributing it to the author of that text, idea or image amounts to theft. Nevertheless, in academia, students have great difficulty with this concept, in part, because they often do not know that plagiarism comes in many different guises – some estimates identify 20 variations. (5) The broad instruction that students should use their own words is often unhelpful because, in many cases, as noted by Ross (6), they lack the skills of summarising and paraphrasing that would enable them to avoid committing plagiarism. However, Williams (7) has suggested that the whole issue of plagiarism raises a more fundamental issue and that is related to critical thinking. As Ivor Scott (8), a well-published academic author frequently cited in academic articles and other texts notes

If imitation is the sincerest form of flattery, then finding my words coming back at me verbatim in my students' essays, should make me exceedingly flattered, but, in fact, makes me incredibly angry. I am not the ultimate authority in my field and I would like to have my words, thoughts and ideas challenged, not copied.

Thus, it is vital that students understand exactly what comprises plagiarism – in all its forms. For academia, there is a duty to ensure that students are trained in the skills of citation, referencing, summarising and paraphrasing at an early stage in their studies. This will mean that they can use the work of others in a responsible way to support their line of reasoning and demonstrate 'the skills of critical thinking that distinguish university education'. (9)

How to lay out the Reference List following the Vancouver Style

1. Fairfull B., Hunter A. Division of labour: the ethical impact. 2nd ed. London: Thames Press; 2009.
2. Scribner A. Authorship by proxy: the case of the non-original best-seller. Prof Ethics 2006 Mar 3; 15(3): 51–59.
3. Cruikshanks R. Working the style [online]. 2012. [Cited 2012 Apr 1]. Available from: URL: http://www.hvn.ac.uk/truth/trickco.htm.
4. Peel R. Wealth by stealth. Melbourne: Outback Press; 1944.
5. Schneider F., Kleister C., Krebs M., Schnecke V. Word for word. Düsseldorf: Rhein Verlag; 2010.
6. Ross F. The power of the pen. Dover: Kentish Press; 2003.
7. Douglas G. Reasoning critically: the ethical way. Richmond: Swaledale Press; 2010.
8. Scott I. editor. The reality of learning. Inverness: Heatherbank Press; 2011.
9. Chatsworth B. Academic education. In: Diddle M. Making the student mind. Edinburgh: Norloch Publishing, 2005; 103–115.

Note: numbers in this list correspond to the figures shown in round brackets at the appropriate point within the text.

Quotations in the text following the Vancouver Style

Short quotations

The movement of words within a sentence or the substitution of a synonym is not sufficient to avoid plagiarism and it is certainly not what could be regarded as 'a summary of the key idea of the text'. (7)

According to Douglas (4) 'stealing another person's ideas is tantamount to stealing their soul'.

If you need to make **a quote within a quote**, then there are two interpretations: British and US American. In the British convention, the long quotation is in single quotation marks and the quotation within that quote is in double quotation marks.

British English version:

The review noted that 'head teachers are taking early retirement as they would rather go on "gardening leave" than face the bureaucracy of constant inspections.'

American English version:

The review noted that "head teachers are taking early retirement as they would rather go on 'gardening leave' than face the bureaucracy of constant inspections."

Long quotations

If the quotation is more than 40 words, then the text of the quotation should be indented by one or two tab spaces from the left-hand margin and amended to single line spacing for that quotation alone.

e.g. It has been found that children in schools are often

... found to be lacking those skills of knowing how to put the ideas of others into their own words without using the source text verbatim. In an age where text messaging invites modifications of language that abbreviate whole words to a single letter or figure, it appears that this skill in brevity has not translated into adequate styles of paraphrasing abstract concepts within academic contexts. (8)

Specific features

In-text citation:

● Numbering should be consecutive throughout the paper. However, if a source is repeated, then the number reference is reused for each occurrence of the repetition, regardless of its previous position in the text. The numbers should be either [3] or (3). Whichever you choose, ensure that you are consistent. These should be placed *after* the full stop (if they are placed at the end of a sentence).

● Where you need to cite a number of references as a group in your text, then use the format: 5,7,9 (without spaces after the comma) but if you have a sequence of references that you wish to re-cite, then for references 4, 5, 6, 7, 8, print 4–8. If there are only two items together, then you need only write 3,4.

- Where more than one work is being cited in relation to the same point, then the reference numbers should appear within one set of brackets, separated by commas: *... a condition that will worsen if neglected (5, 9)*.
- In many medical journals, the in-text number is printed as superscript[#].
- If the citation is a direct quote, then the page number should be given. The abbreviation used for page(s) is **p.** in this style.
- If the author's name is used in the text, then it should be followed immediately by the number of the reference, thus: *As Adamson (8) claimed ...*

Reference list

The Vancouver Style is claimed to demand less punctuation, spacing and formatting than other styles which makes the citations less intrusive of the text. Thus, italicisation or underlining is not used for titles. Capital letters are only used for the initial word apart from proper nouns – people, organisations and places. No full stops between initials for first names of authors.

Note journals have different formats:

- Day, month, year | Month, year | Season and year | Year only.

Where a journal article has seven or more authors, the first six authors are given in the reference list and et al. is added. Note that including et al. in the reference list differs from the convention in other referencing styles.

In some variations of the Vancouver Style, especially in medical journals:

- the place of publication and the publisher are given in publisher/ place of publication order;
- abbreviations are used for journal titles e.g. **Journal of Professional Ethics** may become **JProfessional Ethics** and the **British Medical Journal** becomes **BMJ**. Further information about medical and biomedical journals can be found at ***http://www.ncbi.nlm.nih.gov/ nlmcatalog/journals*** (replaces PubMed Journals Database);
- punctuation conventions may vary considerably.

Even if you have been advised to use the Vancouver Style, you should check in your handbook or guidelines to ensure that you follow the interpretation of that style as described there.

How to list different types of source following the Vancouver Style

Some interpretations of the Vancouver Style use a semi-colon between the publisher and the date; other interpretations use a comma. For the purposes of this publication, the semi-colon has been used.

Hard copy resources	# denotes the number of the citation within the text.
Book by one author	# Graham FK. Ethical dilemmas in academia. 4th ed. Perth: Fair City Press; 2007.
Book by two authors	# Fairfull BM, Hunter AS. Division of labour: the ethical impact. London: Thames Press; 2009.
Book with seven or more authors	# Schneider FJ, Kleister CK, Krebs M, Schnecke V, Dohman, W, Rotenberg K, et al. Word for word. Düsseldorf: Rhein Verlag; 2010.
Book under editorship	# Scott I, editor. The reality of learning. Inverness: Heatherbank Press; 2011.
Chapter in a book	# Chatsworth B. Academic education. In: Diddle MK, editor. Making the student mind. 2nd ed. Edinburgh: Norloch Publishing; 2005. p.103–15.
Secondary referencing – where the original text is not available and the reference relates to a citation in a text which you have read	Imagine that the book you wish to cite was by Williams published in 1996 and cited in Douglas published in 2010. The book by Douglas is the book you actually read. In the Vancouver style you would cite only Williams in the text, thus: Williams # suggests that there is little point in mounting campaigns against plagiarism if there is no real understanding of the principles of paraphrasing. In the reference list you would list this as follows: # Williams WK. Convincing paraphrasing. Med Educ 1996; 12: 140–155. In: Douglas G. Reasoning critically: the ethical way. Richmond: Swaledale Press; 2010.
Journal article	# Scribner A. Authorship by proxy: the case of the non-original best-seller. J Prof Ethics 2006 Dec 20; 33(4): 51–9.
Conference paper	# Anderson JJ. Current developments in language learning by scientists. In: Spratt J., Taylor T., editors. Proceedings of the 5th Convention of Scientific Translators; 2009: Glasgow, UK: Scottish Association of Linguists; 2010. p. 56–63.
Newspaper articles (A = column)	# Gifford, K. Summarising symptoms: the skill of writing summaries. Taymouth Chronicle. 2012 Feb 2; A:4.

Continued overleaf

Online resources	
Internet references including e-books	# Cruikshanks R. Working the style [book on the internet]. Gosport: Hampshire Press; 2012 [cited 2012 Apr 1]. Available from: http://www.hvn.ac.uk/truth/trickco.htm.
Journal article online	(#) Lindsay MD. The dialogue of citation: building the argument. J Ethical Enquiries 2007 [cited 2012 December 4]; 320; [about 12 screens]. Available from: http://www.ethicalenquiries.com/content/lindsay/192445.
Journal article	# Kay, J., 2008. Plagiarism detection: is it a good use of academic time? Journal of the New Age [Internet], 2008 October 23; [cited 2010 January 14]; 2 (3): 200–7. Available from: http://www.jna.org/vol2/issue3/200.html.
Wiki	Since wiki content is usually generated by multiple users, usually no author is named. Vancouver Style does not appear to date to provide a view on citing this developing technology. A comprehensive range of wiki types and how to cite them is available at: http://www.ncbi.nlm.nih.gov/books/NBK7266/#A61262.
Website known author	# Dysart, RM. Stealing the idea or stealing the text [Internet]. [Place unknown]: Effective Editor Associates; 2007 [updated 2009 Feb 14; cited December 2011]. Available from: http://www.effectiveeditor.com.
Website unknown author	# Intercontinental Plagiarism Detection and Compliance Board [Internet]. Georgetown: [cited 2010 14 2011]. Available from: http://www.ipdcb.org.
Online newspaper	# Health professionals fear for future of handwritten notes. Tayside Mail [Internet]. 2011 May 17 [cited 2011 Jun 5]. Available from: http://www.taysidemail.com/news/health/education/health-professionals-fear-for-future-of-handwritten-notes/.
Video-recordings	# Presenting and producing: writers of the future. [DVD]. Venice: Gondola Productions; 2012.
Email communication	Emails are regarded as 'personal communication' and therefore it is expected that you will ask permission to cite an email from the person who sent it. Yorke, A. Finding online resources for project. [Internet.] Message to: Rob Burns. 2011 August 26 [cited 2012 Jan 25]. 2 paragraphs.
Blog	# Shelley B. The write right blog [Internet]. Stratford (UK): Bobbie Shelley; 2011 [cited 2011 Nov 5]. Available from: http://fountainpen.blogspot.com/.

Appendix 1 GRAMMAR TOOLKIT

Definitions to help you seek more information

Grammar term	Definition/model	Example
adjective	*Describes* nouns or gerunds.	A <u>red</u> book; an <u>innovative</u> project.
adverb	Adds information as to *how* something is done.	The student read <u>quickly</u>.
articles	There are only three in English: *a, an, the*. There are particular rules about using these and you will find these in a grammar book.	A shot in the dark; an empty house; the Highway Code.
clause	Part of sentence containing a verb. If the verb and the words relating to it can stand alone, then they comprise the *main clause*. If the words cannot stand alone, then the verb and the words that go with it form a *subordinate clause*.	Cats eat mice <u>which are vermin</u>. Main clause subordinate clause
conditional	Used to explain future possible situation, note the comma after the condition.	If I had the time, I <u>would</u> go out. condition consequence
conjunction	Word that joins two clauses in a sentence where the ideas are connected or equally balanced.	The book was on loan <u>and</u> the student had to reserve it.
demonstratives	There are four in English: *this, these; that, those*.	<u>This</u> house supports the abolition of smoking in public.
direct object	The noun or pronoun which is affected by the verb.	Foxes kill <u>sheep</u>. Foxes eat <u>them</u>.

Continued overleaf

Grammar term	Definition/model	Example
future tense	Explaining things that have not yet happened. There are two forms: *'will'* or *'shall'* and *'going to'*.	I *shall work* until I am 65. They *will come* early. He is *going to* work harder.
gerunds	The gerund acts as a noun and is formed with the part of the verb called the present participle: ... *-ing*.	*Speaking* is easier than *writing* for most people.
indirect object	The person or thing that benefits from the action of a verb. ('to' is understood and not written.)	Tutors give (to) *students* written work. They give (to) *them* essays.
infinitive	Sometimes called the simple or root form of the verb. This form is usually listed in dictionaries, but without 'to'.	e.g. to work.
nouns	Term used to refer to things or people. There are different types: e.g. *abstract* (non-visible), *concrete* (visible) and *proper nouns* (names of people, places, organisations, rivers, mountain ranges).	Abstract nouns: *imagination, thought.* Concrete nouns: *chair, table.* Proper nouns: *Caesar, Rome, the Post Office, the Rhine, the Andes.*
passive voice	Used to describe things objectively, that is, placing the emphasis of the sentence on the action rather than the actor. Although some electronic grammar checkers imply that the passive is wrong. It is perfectly correct. Often used in academic writing (see p. 65 and p. 120).	*Essays are written* by students. Action Actor
past participle	This is usually formed by adding *-ed* to the verb stem. However, in English there are many irregular verbs. You will find lists of these verbs in many dictionaries.	*Worked* **but** many irregular verbs e.g. *bent, drunk; eaten, seen; thought; understood.*

Grammar term	Definition/model	Example
phrasal verbs	These verbs have a particle or particles (see prepositions) as one of their components. These verbs are generally regarded as being less formal in tone than single word verbs.	_Set down_ (deposit), _pick up_ (collect), _write down_ (note), _look out for_ (observe).
possessives	Words indicating ownership: _my, mine, your, yours, his, her, its, our, ours, their, theirs._	_My_ house and _his_ are worth the same. _Mine_ is larger but _his_ has more land.
prepositions	Words used with nouns. Sometimes these are followed by an article (a, an, the), sometimes not, e.g. _at, by, in, for, from, of, on, over, through, under, with._	Put money _in_ the bank _for_ a rainy day or save it _for_ summer holidays _in_ the sun.
present participle	This is formed by adding -_ing_ to the simple verb form. It is used to form continuous verb tenses.	The sun is _setting_. We were _watching_ the yachts.
pronouns	Words used instead of nouns: _I, me, you, he, him, she, her, it, we, us, they, them._ Also words such as: _each, everyone._	_I_ have given _it_ to _him_. _We_ gave _them_ information for _him_.
relative pronouns	Words which link adjective clauses to the noun about which they give more information: _that, which, who, whose, whom._	This is the house _that_ Jack built. Jack, _who_ owns it, lives there. Jack, _whose_ wife sings, is a baker. Jack, to _whom_ we sold the flour, used it to bake bread.
sentence	The smallest grouping of words, one of which must be a verb, which can stand together independently and make sense.	The people elect their leaders in a democracy.
subject	The person or thing that performs the action in a sentence.	_Caesar_ invaded Britain. _Caterpillars_ eat leaves.

Continued overleaf

Grammar term	Definition/model	Example
tense	In English, to show past, present and future tense shifts, the verb changes. This often involves adding a word to show this. Some verbs behave irregularly from the standard rules. Here are three basic tenses; more can be found in a grammar book or language learner's dictionary.	**Simple Past** I studied we studied you studied you studied s/he studied they studied **Present** I study we study you study you study s/he studies they study **Future** I will study we will study you will study you will study s/he will study they will study
topic introducer (TI)/ sentence (TS)	The first sentence in a paragraph introduces the key point of the text; the topic (second) sentence explains the paragraph content.	*Skiing is a popular sport. (TI) Skiers enjoy this in winter on real snow and in summer on dry slopes. (TS)*
verb	The action or 'doing' word in a sentence. It changes form to indicate shifts in time (see tense) and who is 'doing' the action (I, you, he/she, it, we, you [plural], they).	*I work, I am working, I will work, I worked, I was working, I have worked, I had worked.*

Error	Incorrect examples (✗) and correction (✓)
1 Comparing Sometimes there is confusion with when to use a word ending in -er or -est rather than using more or most. For grammar book entry, look for **Comparatives** and **Superlatives**	*Comparing two things:* ✗ The debit was more bigger than the credit. ✓ The debit was **greater** than the credit. *Comparing three or more things:* ✗ China has the most greatest population in the world. ✓ China has the great<u>est</u> population in the world. *Countable and non-countable:* ✗ There were less cases of meningitis last year. ✓ There were **fewer** cases of meningitis last year. (**Countable**) ✗ There was fewer snow last year. ✓ There was **less** snow last year. (**Non-countable**)
2 Describing Commas are vital to meaning where a 'wh-' clause is used. For grammar book entry, look for **Relative clauses**	✗ Toys, which are dangerous, should not be given to small children. (Inference: all toys are dangerous – not what author means.) ✓ Toys which are dangerous should not be given to small children. (Inference: only safe toys should be given to children – what the author means.)
3 Encapsulating Using one word to represent a previous word or idea. For grammar book entry, look for **Demonstrative pronoun**	✗ ... impact of diesel use on air quality. **This** increases in rush-hour. ✓ ... impact of diesel use on air quality. **This impact** increases in rush-hour. or ✓ ... impact of diesel use on air quality. **This use** increases in rush-hour. or ✓ ... impact of diesel use on air quality. **This air quality** increases in rush-hour. (Be sure that the word 'this' or 'these', 'that' or 'those' represents is identifiable by using a general noun that encapsulates the idea – in this case 'impact'.)

Continued overleaf

Error	Incorrect examples (✗) and correction (✓)
4 Its/it's These two phrases are often confused. For grammar book entry, look for **Possessives** (its) and **Apostrophes** or **Contractions** (it's)	✗ As it's aim, the book describes the whole problem. ✓ As its aim, the book describes the whole problem. (possession) ✗ Its not a viable answer to the problem. ✓ It's not a viable answer to the problem (It is …) ✗ Its not had a good review. ✓ It's not had a good review. (It has …)
5 Joining Words such as 'because', 'but' and 'and' join two clauses, they should not be used to begin sentences. For grammar book entry, look for **Conjunctions**	✗ Because the sample was too small, the results were invalid. ✓ The results were invalid because the sample was too small. ('Because' is a conjunction and is used to join two ideas.) ✗ But the UN failed to act. And the member states did nothing. ✓ The country was attacked, **but** the UN failed to act **and** the member states did nothing. ('but' and 'and' are conjunctions that join two separate ideas)
6 Double negative Two negatives mean a positive. Sometimes using a double negative can cause confusion. For grammar book entry, look for **Double negatives**	✗ They have **not** had **no** results from their experiments. ✓ They have not had any results from their experiments. ✗ The government had **not** done **nothing** to alleviate poverty. ✓ The government had done nothing to alleviate poverty.
7 Past participles These are sometimes misused, especially when the verbs are irregular. For grammar book entry, look for **Past participles**	✗ The team had went to present their findings at the conference. ✓ The team had gone to present their findings at the conference.
8 Preposition These should not come at the end of a sentence. For grammar book entry, look for **Prepositions**	✗ These figures are the ones you will work **with**. ✓ These figures are the ones **with which** you will work.

Error	Incorrect examples (✗) and correction (✓)
9 Pronouns These are used to replace nouns. The singular pronouns often cause confusion because they need to agree with the verb. For grammar book entry, look for **Pronouns**	**Singular pronouns** – anybody, anyone, anything, each, either, everybody, everyone, everything, neither, nobody, no-one, nothing, somebody, someone, something take a singular verb. ✗ Each of the new measures are to be introduced separately. ✓ Each of the new measures **is** to be introduced separately. **Reflexive pronouns** ✗ Although disappointed, they only have theirselves to blame. ✓ Although disappointed, they only have **themselves** to blame.
10 Specifying Words that are used to identify specific singular and plural items must match. For grammar book entry, look for **Demonstratives**	✓ **This** kind of mistake **is** common. (Singular demonstrative and verb) ✓ **These** kinds of mistakes **are** less common. (Plural demonstrative and verb) But ✓ **That** result **is** acceptable. (Singular demonstrative and verb) ✓ **Those** results **are** not acceptable. (Plural demonstrative and verb)
11 Subject–verb agreement Often singular subjects are matched with plural verbs and vice versa. For grammar book entry, look for **Subject–verb agreement**	✗ The Principal, together with the Chancellor, were present. ✓ The **Principal**, together with the Chancellor, **was** present. ✗ It is the result of these overtures and influences that help to mould personal identity. ✓ It is the **result** of these overtures and influences that **helps** to mould personal identity.
12 There/Their/They're These simply need to be remembered. For grammar book entry, look for **Words that are often confused** or **homophomes**. Note 'they're' is a contraction of 'they are'. Contractions are not usually used in academic writing.	✗ They finished there work before noon. ✓ **They** finished **their** work before noon. (Shows possession) ✗ We have six places at the conference. We'll go their. ✓ We have six places **at the conference**. We'll go **there**. (Shows location) ✗ Researchers are skilled but there not highly paid. ✓ **Researchers** are skilled but **they're** not highly paid. (They are ....)

Appendix 3 RULES OF PUNCTUATION
Usage for citing and referencing

In citing and referencing, punctuation marks are used in different ways depending on the style that is being followed. The highlighted areas in the table indicate this special usage. Check the style you need for specific features involving punctuation **Chapters 11–15**.

Punctuation	Mark	How the mark is used
Apostrophe	... '	• For possession: e.g. *Napoleon's armies* (singular owner) *Students' essays* (plural owner) • For contraction: e.g. *Don't cry; I'm hungry; it's late* **But note:** *As **its** central theme, the book considered wind power* (no apostrophe required at **its**). Use of the apostrophe is less common in academic writing. For example, some academics would be less comfortable with: *Hospital stay patients' difficulties with the effects of clostridium difficile are not well-documented.* Preference might be for: *The difficulties of hospital stay patients with the effects of clostridium difficile are not well-documented.*
Brackets (parenthesis)	[...] (...)	• Square brackets [...]: for adding words within a quote. • Round brackets (...): to isolate explanatory information. • Both used in citing and reference list for: dates, page numbers. Varies across styles.
Capital letter	ABC	• Starts sentences, proper nouns, seasons, rivers, mountain ranges, places, Acts of Parliament, titles, organisations. • First word only in some styles; all significant title words in other styles.

Punctuation	Mark	How the mark is used
Colon	:	• Divides statements of equal importance. e.g. *I hate maths; he loves it.* • Introduces lists. • Introduces a 'long quote'; depends on wording of the preceding sentence. • Used to separate elements in the reference list. Varies across styles.
Comma	...,	• Separates items in a list of three or more e.g. *tea, beer, juice and wine.* • Separates part of a sentence e.g. *He came home, ate and fell asleep.* • Separates additional information within a sentence e.g. *Rugby, in the main, is a contact sport.* • Marks adverbs e.g. *Certainly, the results have been positive.* • Used to separate elements in the reference list. Varies across styles.
Dash	–	• Marks an aside/addition e.g. *Murder – regardless of reason – is a crime.*
Ellipsis	...	• Marks words omitted from a quotation e.g. *'taxes ... mean price rises'.*
Exclamation mark	!	• Shows shock, horror. Rarely used in academic writing e.g. *Help!*
Full stop	.	• Marks the end of a sentence e.g. This is the end. • Marks an abbreviation e.g. *Prof., etc., i.e., m.p.h., p.a.* • Used to mark separation between elements of reference. Styles vary.
Hyphen	-	• Joins a single letter to an existing word e.g. *x-ray.* • Separates prefixes e.g. *post-modern.* • Prevents repetition of certain letters e.g. *semi-independent.* • Joins a prefix to a proper noun e.g. *pro-British.* • Creates a noun from a phrasal verb e.g. *show-off.* • Joins numbers and fractions e.g. *Twenty-three; three-quarters.* • Triple hyphens used to mark repetition of an author's name in reference list in some styles.

Punctuation	Mark	How the mark is used
Italics	*italics*	• Differentiates text to show quotations, titles of publications in citations, species, works of art, foreign words e.g. *déjà vu; et al.* • Used in some styles in referencing for titles of books, journal articles.
Question mark	?	• Ends sentences that ask a direct question. e.g. *Who am I?* • If question mark is in original quote, then include it in the quotation in the text.
Quotation marks (inverted commas)	' ... ' " ... "	• 'Single quotation marks' mark exact words spoken/printed in a text. • "Double quotation marks" place a quotation within a quotation (British English). • Note that in some word-processing packages it is possible to choose between 'curly quotes' (" ... ") and 'straight quotes' (" ... "). • Used in some referencing styles to enclose article or chapter titles. Check Chapters 11–15 for specific features. • Special use in quotation layouts for each style. See Chapters 11–15.
Semi-colon	;	• Separates two or more clauses of equal importance e.g. *They won the battle; the other side won the war.* • Separates listed items especially when description uses several words. • Used in some styles to separate reference list elements. See Chapters 11–15 for details.

Appendix 4 TWENTY BASIC SPELLING RULES

In English the 'rules' are difficult to define because frequently there are exceptions to them. Here are some of the fundamental rules with some examples of exceptions where these occur.

Number	Rule	Examples with exceptions as applicable
Rule 1	*'i'* comes before *'e'* (except **after** *'c'*)	*belief, chief, relief, science, sufficient* **but** *ceiling, deceive, leisure, perceive, receive, seize, vein, weird*
Rule 2	**Verbs:** where verbs end in *-eed* and *-ede*, then the *-eed* ending goes with *suc-/ex-/pro-*; *-ede* applies in all other cases	*-eed: succeed, exceed, proceed* *-ede: precede, concede*
Rule 3	**Verbs:** where verbs end with *-ise*, nouns end with *-ice*	*practise* (verb)/*practice* (noun) **but** *exercise*: verb and noun
Rule 4	**Double letters** **Double** final consonants before using *-ing* when the words are single syllable and end with *b/d/g/m/n/p/r/t* **Double** consonant when the stressed syllable is at the end of the word **Double 'l'** when words end in an *'l'* preceded by a short vowel	 *robbed, ridding, bagging, summing, running, hopper, furred, fittest* *occurred, beginning, forgettable* *travelled, levelled*
Rule 5	**NOUNS** ending in *'-our'*, drop the *'u'* in the adjective form	*glamour/glamorous*; *humour, humorous*

Continued overleaf

Number	Rule	Examples with exceptions as applicable
Rule 6	**Plurals** generally add '-s' or '-es' after -ss/x/ch/sh/	boys, cats, dogs; crosses, fixes, churches, dishes
	Nouns ending in -y drop -y and add -ies	ally/allies; copy/copies **but** monkeys; donkeys
	Nouns ending in -o, then add -s for the plural	photos; pianos **but** tomatoes; volcanoes; heroes
	Nouns ending in -f and -fe, no consistent rule.	Chief/chiefs **but** half/halves
	Some 'foreign' nouns follow the rules of their own language	Bureau/bureaux; criterion/criteria; datum/data; medium/media.
	Hyphenated words	brothers-in-law; commanders-in-chief
	Some nouns are the same format for singular and for plural	sheep, fish
Rule 7	**Prefixes** dis- and mis- do not add extra letters	dis+agree, mis+manage, Note dis+satisfaction/dissatisfaction, mis + spell/mis-spell
Rule 8	**Suffixes** -ful, -fully, -al, -ally: adjectives formed with the suffix 'ful' and 'al' have only one 'l'	careful; hopeful **but** carefully and hopefully
	When forming adverbs, add -ly	skilfully, marginally
	Adjectives ending in -ic form their adverbs with -ally	basic/basically
Rule 9	**Compound words** where there is a double 'l' in one of the words, one 'l' may be dropped.	full + fill = fulfil; hope + full = hopeful
Rule 10	**Silent** 'e' usually keep -e when adding the suffix	hope + full = hopeful
	If suffix begins with a vowel, the drop final -e	come + ing = coming
	After words ending in -ce or -ge, keep -e to keep sounds soft	noticeable, courageous
Rule 11	For words ending in -y that are preceded by a consonant, change -y to -i before any suffix except -ing, -ism, -ish	dry/driest **but** drying, copyist, cronyism, dryish
Rule 12	For words ending in -ic, or -ac, add -k before -ing, -ed, or -er	trafficking; mimic/mimicked; picnic/picnicker
Rule 13	For joins within word, do not add or subtract letters at 'join'	meanness

Number	Rule	Examples with exceptions as applicable
Rule 14	Silent letters	*debt*, **g***nat*, **k***not*, *palm*, **p***sychiatrist*, **w***rong*
Rule 15	Latin words in English ending in *-ix* in the singular, end in *-ices* in the plural	*appendix, appendices; index, indices*
Rule 16	Latin words in English ending in *-um* in the singular, end in *-a* in the plural	*datum, data; medium, media; stratum, strata*
Rule 17	Latin words in English ending *-us* in the singular, end in *-i* in the plural	*radius, radii*
Rule 18	Latin words in English ending in *-a* in the singular, end in *-ae* in the plural	*agenda, agendae; formula, formulae*
Rule 19	Greek words in English ending in *-ion* in the singular, end in *-ia* in the plural	*criterion, criteria*
Rule 20	Greek words in English ending in *-sis* in the singular, end in *-ses* in the plural	*analysis, analyses; hypothesis, hypotheses*

LIST OF REFERENCES

The following websites have been cited in this book

Ch 1	Macmillan Online Dictionary, Avaiable at: www.macmillandictionary.com [Accessed 27 March 2012].
Ch 2	Joint Nature Conservation Committee. Avaiable at: http://jncc.defra.gov.uk/page-5-theme=textonly http://jncc.defra.gov.uk/page-2 http://jncc.defra.gov.uk/pdf/rs_releaseadvicenote.pdf [Accessed 30th January 2012].
	Websites listed as sources: • http://safeassign.com/ • www.grammarly.com • http://submit.ac.uk (turnitin uk)
Ch 3	University of Dundee 2005 Code of Practice on Plagiarism and Academic Dishonesty [online] Available at: www.dundee.ac.uk/academic/plagiarism.htm [Accessed 1 March 2012].
	BBC News Website. Available at: http://www.bbc.co.uk/news/uk-england-cambridgeshire-16785217 [Accessed 30th January 2012].
	Merriam-Webster Online Dictionary 2011. Available at: nws.merriam-webster.com/opendictionary [Accessed 27th March 2012].
	Longman Dictionary of Contemporary English 2011. Available at: www.ldoceonline.com [Accessed 27th March 2012].
	Macmillan Online Dictionary. Available at: www.macmillandictionary.com [Accessed 27th March 2011].
Ch 4	Imperial College London Reference Management Software Comparison. Available at: https://workspace.imperial.ac.uk/library/Public/Reference_management_software_comparison.pdf [Accessed 1st February 2012].
	McMillan, K. and Weyers, J., 2012.The Study Skills Book. 3rd edition. Harlow: Pearson Education.
	Britannica Online. Available at: http://www.britannica.com/EBchecked/topic/182308/election/229019/Plebiscite [Accessed 17th February 2012].
	Wikipedia. Available at: http://en.wikipedia.org/wiki/Referendum [Accessed 17th February 2012].

	Websites listed as sources: • Web of Science/Web of Knowledge. Available at: www.webofknowledge.com [Accessed 17 February 2012]. • Scifinder. Available at: www.cas.org [Accessed 17 February 2012]. • Medline®. Available at: www.nlm.nih.gov [Accessed 17 February 2012].
Ch 5	nil
Ch 6	Garfield, E., 1997. Concept of citation indexing. Available at: www.garfield.library.upenn.edu/papers/vladivostok.html [Accessed 24th March 2012].
Ch 7	nil
Ch 8	Intellectual Property Office 2009. Available at: www.ipo.gov.uk/c-benefit.htm [Accessed 12th March 2012].
Ch 9	nil
Ch 10	European Union English Style Guide. Available at: ec.europa.eu/translation/english/guidelines/documents/styleguide_ english_dgt_en.pdf [Accessed 14th February 2012].
	Australian Style Manual. Available at: http://australia.gov.au/publications/ style-manual [Accessed 14th February 2012].
	Canadian Guide to Uniform Legal Citation, 7th Edition/Manuel canadien de la référence juridique, 7e edition Available at: www.carswell.com [Accessed 14 February 2012].
	British Standards Institution. Information and documentation — Guidelines for bibliographic references and citations to information resources. London: BSI, 2010 (BS ISO 690).
	British Standards Institution. *Recommendations for citing and* *referencing published materials.* London: BSI, 1990 (BS 5605).
	British Standards Institution. *Recommendations for citation of* *unpublished documents.* London: BSI, 1983 (BS 6371).
	Economic and Social Data Service. Available at: www.esds.ac.uk/ international/access/citing.asp [Accessed 14th February 2012]
	The Blue Book A Uniform System of Citation® for US Legal Citations. Available at: www.legalbluebook [Accessed 16 February 2012].
	ALWD Citation Manual (for citation of legal documents). Available at: www.alwd.org [Accessed 16 February 2012].

Ch 11	American Psychological Association (APA) Style. Available at: http://www.library.cornell.edu/resrch/citmanage/apa [Accessed 28 March 2012].
	American Psychological Association (APA) Style. Available at: http://owl.english.purdue.edu [Accessed 28 March 2012].
	American Psychological Association (APA) Style. Available at: http://psychology.vanguard.edu/faculty/douglas-degelman/apa-style/ [Accessed 28 March 2012].
	American Psychological Association (APA) Style. Available at: http://www.unc.edu/courses/2005fall/engl/012/025/Handouts/APA_films.pdf [Accessed 28 March 2012].
Ch 12	Chicago Style. Available at: http://www.chicagomanualofstyle.org/home.html [Accessed 25 March 2012].
Ch13	Harvard Style. Available at: http://www.lc.unsw.edu.au/onlib/ref_elec2.html [Accessed 26 February 2012].
	Harvard Style. Available at: http://home.ched.coventry.ac.uk/caw/harvard/ [Accessed 26 February 2012].
	Harvard Style. Available at: http://www.bournemouth.ac.uk/library/citing_references/citing_refs_main.html [Accessed 26 February 2012].
Ch 14	Modern Languages Association Style. Available at: www.uhv.edu/ac/style/MLAQuickGuide.pdf [Accessed 29 March 2012].
	Modern Languages Association Style. Available at: www.mla.org [Accessed 29 March 2012].
	Modern Languages Association Style. Available at: http://owl.english.purdue.edu/handouts/research/r_mla.html [Accessed 29 March 2012].
Ch 15	Vancouver Style. Available at: http://www.bma.org.uk/library_services [Accessed 26 March 2012].
	Vancouver Style. Available at: http://www.monash.edu.au [Accessed 26 March 2012].
	Vancouver Style. Available at: http://www.ncbi.nlm.nih.gov/books/NBK7266/#A61262 [Accessed 26 March 2012].
	Vancouver Style. Available at: www.library.vcc.ca/downloads/VCC/VancouverStyleGuide.pdf [Accessed 26 March 2012].

GLOSSARY

Note that where a word can act as a noun or a verb, for clarity, the role has been given for the word as used in the context of discussion about academic writing and conventions.

Abstract (noun) A short overview of the key methods, ideas and conclusions discussed in the text.

Academic dishonesty Any form of contravention of the academic conventions surrounding the production of academic text or other artefacts. This can include cheating in examinations, plagiarism or falsifying data.

Active voice (gram.) This is used when the actor has equivalent or greater importance than the action in a sentence. For example: *The w*riter [the actor] *used too many quotations in this text* [action]. Compare with 'passive voice'.

Ampersand (&) An abbreviation for *'and'* which is used in some citation styles, but is generally discouraged in academic writing as too informal.

Arts Subjects studied to develop the mind in a particular way. Includes history, languages and literature.

Authorities Experts in an area whose published work has been widely accepted as reflecting detailed command of the area in which they write.

Attribute (verb) To give recognition to the source of information used in an academic text.

Bibliography Dependent on discipline, this can mean either (1) all the literature read on a subject but not necessarily cited in the text or (2) the literature cited in the text.

Caveat **(Latin)** This translates as 'let him beware'. Used in the academic context it is an indication of advice suggesting caution.

Citation (1) The act of making reference to another source in one's own writing. (2) A passage or quotation from another source repeated word for word within a text.

Cogent Coherent or rational.

Colloquial Conversational.

Colon (gram.) A punctuation symbol consisting of two dots one above the other (:) and used, in the context of this book, to introduce long quotes and to separate date and page number in some citation styles.

Conjecture A surmise or view based on inconclusive evidence.

Connotation Implication.

Copyright (noun) The exclusive legal ownership of intellectual property, for example, text, music or artistic work. Those wishing to use this kind of property must pay and/or acknowledge the copyright holder for permission to do so. Copyright is sometimes held by the author; sometimes by the publisher and sometimes by both.

Critical thinking The ability to evaluate opinion and evidence systematically, clearly and with purpose.

Direct speech The words actually spoken by the speaker.

Ellipsis The replacement of words deliberately omitted from quoted text by three dots e.g. 'E-books are offered online … as cheap alternatives to the paperback novel.'

Encyclopaedia A source book of information, explanations and definitions of all branches of knowledge. Plural of 'encyclopaedia' is 'encyclopaedias'. Note: alternative spelling – encyclopedia/encyclopedias.

Eponym Something that is named or thought to be named after the individual who first identified or articulated the characteristics of, for example, a law or syndrome.

Function (noun) The purpose that is being achieved; in academic writing this can be describing, asserting, contending or refuting, for example.

Gravitas **(Latin)** Implied added weight in the sense of seriousness, solemnity, or importance.

Humanities Subjects relating to human life and ideas. Includes ancient and modern languages, literature, history, philosophy, religion, visual and performing arts.

Indices A listing of publications produced at regular intervals, often grouped by subject and in alphabetical order thereafter, that gives bibliographical information and may also include brief summaries (abstracts) of the items listed. The singular of 'indices' is 'index'.

Intellectual property (IP) Any writing, or other abstract work or invention created by an individual and thus owned exclusively by them and which, therefore, cannot be made, copied or sold by another.

Inverted commas This is a term used interchangeably with 'quotation marks'. Single inverted commas look like this: ' ... ' and double inverted commas look like this: " ... ".

Journal A periodical (see below).

Literature In the academic world, the expression 'the literature' usually means the publications authored by subject experts based on their own work in a particular discipline or field.

Objectivity Having a view or approach based on a balanced consideration of the facts.

Nuance Delicate shade of meaning.

Paper mills These are provided by the growing online industry that invites students and others at all levels of study to pay for academic texts that meet their requirements.

Parenthetical Describing the words that may be placed within brackets or parentheses, (...), for example, in some citation styles.

Paraphrasing Restating the key ideas of a text, giving sense, idea or meaning and in other words but in more detail than in summarising.

Passive voice (gram.) This is used when the action is regarded as more important than the actor. For example: *Quotations were over-used in this text* [action] (*by the writer* [actor]). Compare with 'active voice'.

Peer review The evaluation of a draft article by a subject expert or experts which endorses or rejects papers submitted for consideration for publication.

Periodical A subject-specific digest of articles written by subject experts and published at regular intervals over a year for an audience drawn from the academic community and practitioners in the field.

Personal pronouns The words that are used instead of nouns are called pronouns; personal pronouns refer to people or things: *I, you, he/she/ it* (1st, 2nd and 3rd persons singular) and *we/you/they* (1st, 2nd and 3rd persons plural).

Plagiarism The use of the work of another person without acknowledgement; the use of wording from the original text without using quotation marks; where an author has depended on text from other sources which then comprises more than ten per cent of the whole paper produced by that author.

Predicate (noun) One of the two main constituents of a sentence or clause, modifying the subject and including the verb, objects, or phrases governed by the verb. For example, the predicate in the following sentence is in bold: *The doctor **examined the patient at the clinic**.*

Primary source Original material that, for example, reports research data, Acts of Parliament, industrial or business reports as published, that is, material that has not been processed or interpreted by others.

Provenance Concerns the source of information or an artefact by identifying its origin and establishing by whom, when and where it was created.

Quotation The use of words taken directly from the text produced by another author and identified by using the punctuation conventions of quotation marks or indentation where a quotation is more than 30 words drawn from the original text.

Quotation marks Sometimes called 'inverted commas', the punctuation symbols that are usually placed round quotations. Single quotation marks look like this: ' ... ' and double quotation marks look like this: " ... ".

References or Reference list The list of all sources cited in the text providing all necessary bibliographical information that would enable the reader to source the original document.

Reflection The process of thinking over ideas about which you have read or events you have experienced in order to analyse, re-evaluate and perhaps readjust your views based on the content or events.

Refuting Rejecting a particular opinion or approach.

Register (gram.) This term describes the levels of formality and informality used in speech or writing.

Sciences Natural sciences include the studies of biology, chemistry, earth science and physics and all their sub-sets; formal sciences include decision theory, game theory, information theory, logic, mathematics, statistics, systems theory, theoretical computing and some aspects of linguistics.

Secondary source Material that has been processed, interpreted or re-cycled in some way by others. An example from within the academic world is the literature review either published independently or as part of a more extensive work.

Seminal works/literature The key literature on which later studies and literature have been based.

sic **(Latin)** This Latin word means 'thus' and is used in brackets [*sic*] within a quotation where the original author has erroneously used a word or made a grammatical mistake to indicate that the author using the quotation is remaining faithful to the original although aware of the error.

Social Sciences Subjects studying interpersonal relationships in society.

Includes anthropology, area studies, communication studies, cultural studies, economics, geography, history, law, linguistics, political science, psychology and technology.

Subject (gram.) In a sentence, the person or thing doing the action signified by the verb.

Subjectivity Having a view or approach based on a personal opinion, not necessarily taking a balanced account of the facts.

Summarising Creating a broad overview of an original piece of text, briefly stating the main idea but using your own words giving less detail than in paraphrasing.

Summary This term is sometimes used in preference to the term 'abstract'; it too provides a short overview of the key methods, ideas and conclusions discussed in the text.

Synonyms Words similar in meaning.

Syntax The way words are used (in their appropriate grammatical forms), especially with respect to their connection and relationship within sentences.

Terminator paragraph The paragraph that brings a section of writing to an ending or conclusion. This may act also as a transition to the following section or paragraph.

Topic paragraph The paragraph, usually the first, that indicates or points to the topic of a section or piece of writing and how it can be expected to develop.

Topic sentence The sentence, usually the first, that indicates or points to the topic of a paragraph and how it can be expected to develop.

Triangulation Consulting the content of more than one source and comparing what is said in each.

Unethical Describing something which is morally wrong.

Value judgement A statement that reflects the views and values of the speaker or writer rather than the objective reality of what is being assessed or considered.

Verb (gram.) The action or 'doing' word in a sentence. A part of speech by which action or state of being is indicated, serving to connect the subject with a predicate. A verb also shows, for example, time shifts by changes in tense i.e. past, present or future.

verbatim **(Latin)** Latin for 'word for word', that is, exactly as printed in the original.

READY FOR

SCHOOL

A Parents' Guide

About the Authors

Margaret Horan and Geraldine O'Brien have been Primary
Teachers for over thirty years. They are both teaching in
Ireland. Margaret has also taught in Switzerland and Nigeria.
This is their first book.

READY FOR SCHOOL

A Parents' Guide

Margaret Horan & Geraldine O'Brien

First published 2006 by
Veritas Publications
7/8 Lower Abbey Street
Dublin 1
Ireland
Email publications@veritas.ie
Website www.veritas.ie

10 9 8 7 6 5 4 3 2 1

ISBN 1 85390 929 7
978 1 85390 929 0 (from January 2007)

Designed and typeset by Paula Ryan
Printed in the Republic of Ireland by Betaprint, Dublin

*Veritas books are printed on paper made from the wood pulp of managed forests. For
every tree felled, at least one tree is planted, thereby renewing natural resources.*

We would like to dedicate this book to our husbands, Hugho and Frank, and to our families.

Contents

Contents

Introduction

Many parents do not live in close-knit communities where grandparents, brothers, sisters and cousins are nearby. When a question or a problem arises, parents often turn to the teacher for advice and support. This book was written to answer some of the questions and concerns that parents have brought to us over the years.

In *Ready for School,* we explore a range of topics: from managing the excitement of the first day to practical suggestions for handling change, from supporting a child's academic capabilities to worries about bullying.

This book looks at the commonplace questions and dilemmas that every parent faces as they support their child's development though the early days of school. It presents real stories about real children and offers sound advice, based on tried and tested practices, honed over many years in our work with young children. We are not experts, but we do have a wealth of experience, both as teachers and as parents.

We hope that our book will:

* Help you to make the transition from home to school easier for your child.

- Ease any anxieties that you may have.
- Enable you to minimise problems.
- Give you confidence in your child's teachers and encourage you to liase with them, realising that they, too, have your child's best interests at heart.
- Guide you through your child's early years in school.

1 Is my Child Ready for School?

The first of September is approaching and in many countries children will be preparing to begin their journey through primary school. It is a new experience for the child and for their family as everybody gets caught up in the excitement as the calendar rolls towards the first day.

It is a very good idea to find out the age profile in the reception class. If the average age of the children is, for example, four years and nine months, the child who is just four may struggle emotionally and socially. In general, maturity is directly related to age, but, of course, children are unique and parents know them best.

Young children today are very articulate. They are surrounded and stimulated by language from a very early age. We adults often inaccurately interpret this fluency in speech as maturity. Young children may do very well academically, but may experience difficulty in developing relationships within the class groups, especially as the children get older. So before you send your child to school, consider their age and maturity carefully.

Parents can help to make the journey through school go smoothly by being aware in advance of some issues that may arise. When a child starts school, they will be moving from a small, more intimate group to one that is larger and more challenging. This chapter will look at some simple preparations that can be made in advance of the first day. It will suggest ways to promote your child's readiness for school and, by proposing some useful tips, help you manage the challenges and allow your child to get the most from their early days at school.

A Step

Sometimes we are so anxious for our children to have a marvellous love affair with school, and we build it up to such a pitch, that the child cannot sleep or eat for a few days before starting. Fear of the unknown scares most adults, so imagine how much greater that fear is for a small child, who cannot reason or foresee what may lie ahead. In order to minimise any fears, it is good to treat the beginning of primary school as just another natural step in your child's life.

Be Aware of your own Attitudes

We ask parents to examine their own memories of school. Each parent will have spent many years in the classroom and, for each person, the experience will have been different. Your child's experience will be different too, as the educational system is constantly changing and developing. However, children take their outlook on school from you so your positive attitude will influence your child and ensure that they start their journey full of confidence. In the same way, a negative attitude may make your child wary and apprehensive. So try not to burden your child with your anxieties. Don't say things like, 'I hated school', or 'I did not like my teacher, but you will love yours', because, by doing that, you are giving out conflicting messages to your child. If your personal experience of school was not a happy one, your child does not need to know.

Attend the Open Day

Prior to the beginning of the new term, many schools now have an open day when parents and children are encouraged to visit and enjoy a short positive experience. If this is available, it provides a wonderful starting point by removing the fear of the unknown for your child. During the open day, they can visit the new classroom, meet their teacher (if possible) and see their surroundings. The teacher may read them a story while the parents wait, maybe in the school hall. This experience is important for a small child, because now they have met their teacher and seen their classroom. This is also a chance for parents to gain reassurance, ask for practical advice and have any questions answered.

Getting Ready Socially and Emotionally

To help to decide if your child is ready socially and emotionally for this new stage, we ask parents to resist the temptation to judge their child by academic ability alone but to try to see the new experience from their child's point of view by considering the following questions:

- Are they ready to be apart from their parents?
- Will they be able to go to the bathroom on their own?
- Can they open their schoolbag, lunchbox and drink?
- Will the teacher understand what the child is saying?
- Can they play simple games with other children?

A child's academic progress will either be enhanced or hindered by what may seem like relatively small factors. However, in our experience, if the social and emotional development is right, everything else falls into place.

Is my Child too Young?

Sometimes parents worry about whether their child is too young to start school but are afraid that they will hinder their advancement if they wait for another year. Barry's story illustrates this dilemma.

Barry

'Off to school in September for Barry,' said Granny, one sunny day in May. 'I'm not sure,' said Mum. 'He'll be very young for the class and I'm thinking of keeping him at home for another year'. 'Nonsense!' said Granny. 'He is as bright as a button and is showing a great interest in books. Why would you hold him back?'

It was the phrase, 'Hold him back', that got to Mum. That evening, she discussed the matter with Dad. They both decided that Barry was brighter, cleverer and more mature than the average child, so off to school he went.

Barry was indeed as bright and as clever as most of his peers, so he had no trouble with the academic work. However, his emotional and social maturity was directly related to his age. Barry struggled to be included in the more mature groups. During free play, Barry's choice of game was rarely accepted. The older boys dominated the games, and Barry was happy to play a minor role. The same thing happened in the playground. Barry loved joining in the games, but was never allowed to be the leader. Sometimes, he tried to negotiate, but the more mature boys always out-manoeuvred him.

Barry thrived in school academically, but not socially or emotionally. He was competing with boys who were six months to a year older than him. As he matured, they also matured, so he had difficulty catching up with them.

The Immature Child

There are exceptions to every rule but, in our experience, maturity is nearly always linked to age. We find that most children are like Barry and that their emotional and social maturity are directly related to chronological age. Because of their age, immature children are likely to have poor organisational skills, are slow to complete tasks, are unable to negotiate and can become upset more easily. Such children prefer strict guidelines of work rather than the freedom to make choices and can be over-anxious to please. They can be easily dominated and will often accept minor roles to be included in the older children's games. In the main, it is important for children to have the average age profile of their classmates and this should be taken into account when making the decision to start school.

Independence Promotes Confidence

To promote social and emotional maturity and to help make starting school an enjoyable experience, we suggest focusing on your child's independence in the following ways:

- Encourage your child to put on and fasten their coat. Practise this lots of times at home. Do not rush or criticise if it is not perfect. Label the coat clearly, as many children have similar coats.
- If your child is unable to tie laces, Velcro fastenings are a great idea.
- A few days before school begins, try on the new uniform. Leave it on for a while. When they need to use the

bathroom, do not help them and see if they can manage the school trousers or skirt on their own. You may find that belts are usually a hindrance – elasticated waists make it easier. Train them to wash their hands after using the toilet and to turn off the tap when they are finished. Children get distressed if they need help in the bathroom at school.

- Put a tissue or a handkerchief in their pocket and make sure that they can use it.
- The less complicated the schoolbag, the better. Teach them to open and close it. Elaborate schoolbags, pencil cases and lunchboxes often cause tears in school. They are a huge distraction and children get very upset if they are damaged.
- Have a trial run at home with the lunchbox a few days beforehand. Sit with your child at the table and observe how they open the lunchbox, the wrapping on a sandwich, the banana or other fruit, the yoghurt and the drink. Resist the urge to help and make any adjustments that you think are necessary.

Physical Skills

A further way to promote your child's readiness for school is to encourage physical skills. These are some of the ways you can assist your child:

- Teach your child to hold a crayon or thick pencil correctly. Let them do lots of drawing: this will help to develop the muscles in their little hands. At this stage, there is no need to teach your child to write numbers or letters. Numbers and letters will not be a problem to the child who comes to school with well-developed hand muscles.

- Colouring in pictures gives great hand control.
- Every child should have a safety scissors at home. They should use it as often as possible, with supervision.
- Familiarise your child with construction, such as Duplo, Lego etc.
- Let your child be responsible for tidying away their own books, toys and games.
- When playing outdoors, teach them how to bounce, throw, kick and catch a ball.

Concentration

Some children find concentration comes easily; others can get easily distracted. While concentration spans grow with age, parents can encourage concentration in the following ways:

- Develop the practice, from an early age, of sitting quietly with the child and telling a story.
- Encourage your child to finish one game before moving on to another.
- Teach your child simple nursery rhymes.

Communication Skills

Like concentration, a child's communication skills will develop over time, but even at this early stage, following a few small tips can help your child enormously in the first days at school:

- Teach your child to give their first name and surname together when asked, as other children in the class may have the same first name.
- Try not to anticipate their requests. The teacher may not understand your child's body language, so asking clearly is important.
- When children get excited, they become animated and, when telling a story, words and sentences run into each other. Adults enjoy this; teachers also enjoy it. However, when they come to school still using baby talk and broken sentences, it can cause them embarrassment and discomfort in school. Jennifer's story illustrates how distressing this can be for a child.

Jennifer

The children took their turns in telling their news in Jennifer's class. She was all excited when her name was called. She stood proudly in front of the class and in a loud, clear voice announced, 'We went on a choo-choo train to visit my Granny and she gave us biccies and sossies' (biscuits and sausages).

Before she could tell any more, the class burst out laughing, which caught the teacher unawares and caused Jennifer to cry. She

could not understand why the children were laughing at her, as her news was not funny. Between the teacher and her parents, Jennifer soon regained her confidence and her family stopped using baby talk with her.

2 How Can I Help my Child to Settle in?

In the previous chapter we looked at some straightforward ways of helping you and your child to prepare in the run-up to their special first day at school. Now the day is here and it can be emotional for all concerned. Teachers appreciate that parents and children may find this first day traumatic. It is natural for any parent to feel worried, but try not to pass your anxieties on to your child. Your child knows when you are anxious and will wonder what is wrong. They have to cope with a lot of new things today, but why Mum or Dad looks so tense and worried should not be one of them.

In this chapter we will explore ways to help to minimise the worries as you negotiate the first day, and all the days that follow, so that the settling-in process is as enjoyable as possible for everyone. We will consider strategies to help with leaving your child for the first time, offer ways to cope with off days, give suggestions for coping with separation anxiety and present tips for working through misunderstandings.

Drop and Go

Things may seem pretty hectic on that first morning, but trust the teacher and be guided by what they advise. It is very reassuring for a small child to see that someone is in control in the midst of the hustle and bustle.

We usually suggest to parents to 'drop and go'. Bring your child in, introduce them and, when you get a signal from the teacher, say 'See you later' in a positive voice and then leave. Don't linger. Teachers are well able to cope with the reluctant child and will settle them very quickly. Children are curious and will be very interested in what is going on. The mature child will understand that school is a necessary part of their life's journey and will trust that you will be back at a given time to collect them.

When a child is tearful and reluctant to stay in the classroom during the first few days, it is unwise and unhelpful to take them home. Giving a child the option of going home makes settling in more difficult. Some children find new experiences challenging and depend on the confidence of the adults to reassure them. Trust the teacher. They want exactly what you want – a happy little boy or girl. We tell parents that if their child does not settle, we will telephone them, but, in our experience, a little distraction nearly always works. By the end of the first week, most children have settled into school and most parents are breathing a happy sigh of relief.

Don't Make Unrealistic Promises

Try not to resort to bribes or negotiations and do not make any false promises at the classroom door. Each child in a classroom has to be considered, so it is unfair to your child to promise them that they can always choose where they will sit, when they may eat lunch or what story will be read.

Do not promise that you will buy them a toy, book or video, or that you will take them for a special treat, because doing this on a regular basis gives the child a very negative impression of school. Broken promises disappoint and upset children. Unless you fully intend to carry them out, do not make any promises at all.

Be Punctual

Be punctual at collection time, especially during the first few weeks. Imagine a small child's anxiety when everyone else is collected except them. Junior classrooms are hives of activity and stimulation during school hours. But when the children are collected at going-home time, the atmosphere in the classroom changes. The room is now empty and quiet. Children wait eagerly for the person who is collecting them, especially over the first few weeks. Sometimes they become fretful if every other child has been collected except them. The once busy, lively classroom is now quiet and the child just wants to be collected, no matter how much the teacher comforts them. If this happens on a regular basis, it upsets the child and they may become insecure. Being punctual builds up the child's confidence in the adult.

Handling an Off Day

All adults have their off days and so do children. We can rationalise this feeling and get on with things. However, when a small child is having an off day, they may announce out of the blue, 'I don't want to go to school today!'

How you handle the first time your child makes this statement is very important. If your child is happy and settled in school, do not over-react or give too much attention to these words. They are probably having an off day, so distraction is the best course of action. Try saying something like, 'Who will we invite to your birthday party?'

or 'We will have to write your letter to Santa soon' or some other topic that will divert attention.

However, if the off day happens on a regular basis and a child is refusing to go to school, parents should examine recent family events very carefully. Something is causing anxiety for the child, maybe an illness or a change within the home. However, if you suspect that something is bothering them in school, the sooner you discuss it with the teacher, the better.

The Child who is Anxious

Children come in all shapes and sizes and so do their personalities. Some appear to be born with a jolly, outgoing disposition while other children are quieter, more thoughtful but equally happy. Some children are anxious and find separation from their parents more frightening than others. They can become overwhelmed by too many sudden changes and love routine and familiarity. Anxious children anticipate problems that may never happen and dread the unknown.

If you think your child might be anxious about school, don't worry. This is perfectly understandable and together with the tools we have already suggested, the following are additional ways to make starting school a little easier:

- As well as introducing the child to the classroom, it is good to familiarise them with the other parts of the school building such as the canteen, the gym and the toilets.
- Introduce them to the teacher a few times before they go to school.

- Before they start, encourage them to play with other children who will be in their year.
- Don't rush or fuss them in the morning.
- Don't establish a school run with neighbours or friends until the child is ready.
- An emotional connection to home may help them to feel more secure – a favourite toy, a photograph or a book.

The Overly Sensitive Child

What a joy it would be if we could wave a magic wand and guarantee our child a journey free of all of the trials of life. Most parents accept that this is impossible. They understand that their child's unique experiences – some happy, some sad, some positive and some negative – will shape the adult that they become. It is our responsibility to watch, protect and guide our child, rejoicing in their happiness and helping them over the hurdles that may come their way.

It would be wonderful for a child if they faced the world without the burden of hypersensitivity. The overly sensitive child perceives insult and intentional hurt around every corner. They often expect things to go wrong. Some parents respond too readily to every whim, sulk, sad face and insecurity that the child expresses. As a result, this child is sometimes shocked and disappointed when they encounter others who do not respond so readily to them.

Teachers can easily identify the genuinely sensitive child and will deal sympathetically with them, but the over-pampered child is not allowed even the slightest upset and expects to be handled like a delicate flower. When a teacher receives a new infant class, it is always very exciting getting to know the children. It does not take long to figure out their little personalities and traits. Each child is like a special plant – the hardy annuals, the resilient roses, a few gentle amaryllis and, occasionally, one orchid, who is not, under any circumstances, to be corrected, disappointed, urged to do something or challenged in any way. When a parent's attention is drawn to such behaviour, they will often defend the child by saying, 'He is very sensitive'.

All children are sensitive. They need nurturing and encouragement in order to blossom. The pampered child is ill-prepared for school. They rarely infringe on other children. They expect the teacher to anticipate all of their needs and to sort out all of their little problems. They are not demanding children. They will sit quietly and expect the teacher to notice that they do not have a green crayon, a spoon for their yoghurt or that their pencil needs to be sharpened. They will not ask the teacher to help them but cannot understand why they do not come to their assistance. This never happened at home. Their every need was anticipated. Expecting to be pampered and humoured continuously is a habit. Parents and teacher need to work together to break the cycle. This will take time and patience. Otherwise, the child will become unpopular with their peers and unhappy in themselves. If a parent fears their child is overly sensitive they should take the following steps:

- Encourage the child to verbalise their needs.
- Try not to anticipate and indulge their every whim: instant gratification is not good for children.
- If your child is upset, comfort them but encourage them to move on. Being disappointed occasionally is part of life's journey.

Talking to the Teacher

Parents have been educating their child for four or five years before they arrive at the school door. When they start school, the teacher joins in this process. The teacher wants your child to be happy. It makes their job more rewarding and creates a positive environment for your child and their peers. Most interaction between parent and teacher is positive. However, a parent may feel unhappy about how the teacher handles an incident involving their child. If such an occasion arises, it is good to bear in mind the following points:

- Always listen to your child, as they are giving you their personal interpretation of an event.
- Approach the teacher with an open mind and problems can usually be settled to everyone's satisfaction.
- Support your child, but realise that there are two sides to every story.
- Teachers are human and fallible, so if an occasional difficulty arises, be understanding.
- Never, ever threaten a child with the teacher by saying, 'Wait until you go to school', or 'Mrs X will sort you out'.

Karl and Ben's story is a good illustration of how misunderstandings can be addressed:

Karl and Ben

Children love making presents for their family, especially for Mum and Dad. Karl was meticulous about his work and was excited about making a Mothers' Day card. He worked very hard, as he wanted the card to be beautiful for his Mum. When he had finished, he knew that she would love it. He admired it and showed it to Ben, who was sitting beside him. To his horror, Ben picked up a crayon and scribbled on his beautiful card. Karl was very upset and could not be comforted.

This was not the first time that Ben had scribbled on another boy's work, so when the teacher was giving out award stickers, she did not give one to Ben. He was furious. 'I didn't want one anyway,' he said. The teacher knew differently and was sure that Ben would have learnt his lesson. On the way home with his Mum, Ben burst out, 'I was in trouble today for nothing! I did nothing and teacher gave all the boys a sticker except me. It's not fair! She's always blaming me!' Ben's Mum was upset on his behalf and was very annoyed with the teacher. The following day, when she collected Ben, she asked the teacher if she could have a word. The teacher invited herself and Ben into the classroom.

Ben's mother was surprised to hear why her child had been reprimanded, but Ben protested his innocence. When the teacher produced the scribbled card, Ben burst out crying, saying, 'It was only an accident and I didn't mean it'. Mum now understood very clearly why Ben did not deserve a sticker.

3 How Do I Handle Tantrums?

Children are very clever and by the time they start school, they know whether or not tantrums work. Most young children will resort to a tantrum at some time, due to their inability to express their feelings or needs. The first time a child throws a full-blown tantrum can be quite horrifying. As they throw themselves on the ground, arms and legs flying, appearing to be on the verge of bursting a blood vessel, it is difficult for parents not to give in to their request. At times, giving in for peace and quiet all around seems the best option.

Having got their own way, the child is calm and happy again, and Mum and Dad breathe a sigh of relief. Unfortunately, the child has learned that tantrums work and when faced with a denied request again, they will repeat the behaviour. Negative behaviour that goes unchecked does not go away and as the child gets older and stronger, the ferocity, duration and frequency of these tantrums will increase, until the beautiful, bubbly, happy child becomes a tyrant.

It is a good idea for parents to have a strategy in place to deal with tantrums so as not to be taken by surprise when faced with the first one. This chapter looks at advance planning and suggests ways to learn from tantrums when they occur.

Be Prepared

Tantrums can give rise to insecurity in parents and they wonder what they are doing wrong. It is important to realise that most children have tantrums, even your beautiful, adorable, smiling baby. They are not a negative reflection on parents, just a burst of frustration and wilfulness on the part of the child.

The ideas that follow form part of the 'being prepared kit', helping a parent to handle a tantrum with complete confidence, leaving the child in no doubt as to who is in charge.

Tantrums need an audience. If the parent says no calmly, explains the reason for saying no and then continues what they have been doing in a composed manner, the tantrum will often wind down.

- Do not negotiate, as a child in a tantrum is not listening.
- Ensure their physical safety at all times. Holding the child firmly often helps.
- Never hit the child. They may feel more resentful later and you will be burdened with guilt.
- As the tantrum subsides, and it will, gently distract the child by suggesting an activity that they love.
- Do not think ill of your child. They love you, but are trying every technique possible to get their own way. Small children are self-centred.
- Tantrums are not an illness. They will pass with patience, kindness, love and understanding.
- Diversion always works better than punishment.
- Acknowledge good behaviour with praise and rewards.

What if the Tantrum Happens in Public?

When a child misbehaves in public, it adds to the embarrassment and the feeling of helplessness for parents. If there are two parents present, one should remove the child to a less public place and deal with it. If you are on your own and surrounded by tut-tutting, child-free adults, you need a strong nerve and great patience:

- If you are shopping, complete your purchases as quickly as possible, request help with bringing your groceries to the car, strap your screaming child into the car and return home.
- Do not discuss the tantrum on the way home.

- Do not be angry.
- When you get home, bring your child into the house. Let them calm down, again ensuring that they get the message that tantrums do not work.
- Negative attention is better than no attention, so do not over-analyse or discuss the tantrum with or in front of the child.

Sulking

Sometimes a small child, instead of throwing a tantrum when they are disappointed or frustrated, will sulk. A sulk is a silent or inactive show of temper or resentment. It can be quite difficult for a parent to ignore the look of distress on a young child's face. But, like tantrums, the more attention that you give to the sulky child, the more they will use this technique.

Adults will know from their dealings with the child the difference between genuine distress and sulking. Always comfort the disappointed child, but our advice is to pretend that you don't notice the sulk and, without an audience, the child will gradually realise that sulking does not work.

The two stories that follow show contrasting ways of handling tantrums and demonstrate the benefits of recognising the warning signals.

Gregory

Gregory was a lovely, happy baby. By the time he was two years old, he was playing contentedly with his toys and loved when little friends came to play. He liked routine. One evening it was bedtime, just when Gregory was at the best part of his game. As Mum bent down to help Gregory tidy his toys away, he turned and, in an instant, worked himself into a full-blown tantrum, stamping, shouting and screaming at Mum: 'Don't touch my toys! Don't touch my toys! Not finished, not finished!' It was the first time Mum had seen this behaviour and initially she was taken aback.

Mum recognised this as a tantrum straightaway. She bent down, held him securely and told him in a firm but kind voice that it was bedtime and that he could play the game tomorrow. Gregory struggled and fought against her and continued to scream, almost frightening his mother. She loved Gregory dearly, but did not want this tantrum repeated. She continued to hold him, but did not negotiate or try to comfort him, as she was aware that he was no longer listening to her.

After what seemed like a very long time, Gregory calmed down and his Mum said in a very soft voice, 'Let's tidy up now, Gregory, and we'll have story time'. Gregory's mother did not show anger or irritation when dealing with him, as she realised this was a huge lesson for him. Subsequent tantrums were not as stormy or long-lasting, as Gregory realised they did not work. When Gregory started school, tantrums were no longer an issue for him.

Bernard

Bernard learned at an early age that tantrums worked. Seeing their son happy was everything to Mum and Dad. The tantrums escalated out of control and Bernard's parents looked forward to him starting school. They hoped that the teacher would solve the problem for them.

It did not take Bernard long to feel the frustration of school. He did not like being kept waiting for anything and always wanted the best game in the room. He only wanted to hear one story: Jack and the Beanstalk. He wanted to be the leader every day and did not like when the teacher praised someone else and not him. He couldn't understand why teacher put him beside James, when he wanted to sit near Thomas and was flabbergasted by how he was always asked to tidy up, just when he was enjoying himself. For a little boy like Bernard, who was used to getting his own way, all this compromise was too much.

After the initial shyness of starting school disappeared, Bernard decided he'd had enough. School had been quite enjoyable on a particular day until the teacher told him that he would have to wait his turn to play with Lego. Why should he have to wait? He always got what he wanted and he wanted the Lego now. The suddenness of his tantrum took the teacher by surprise. Initially, it also surprised the other children and some were a little frightened. The teacher reassured the other children that Bernard was not really upset, just very cross, and turning to him she said in a clear voice, 'Bernard, you will get the Lego when it is your turn'. Bernard continued to shout and stamp. The teacher appeared to ignore Bernard. She ensured that he was safe and kept him in her *sight at all times. Other children kept a sharp eye on Bernard, just in case he succeeded in his demands. They had sometimes used this technique themselves, to get their own way. The teacher waited just long enough for Bernard to get the message that tantrums did not work in school. She began reading Jack and the Beanstalk. Before long, she noticed that Bernard was showing an interest in his favourite story. When he had exhausted himself and his tantrum, he shuffled back to his place where he had a much better view of the pictures in the book. Without comment, the teacher continued to read and finish the story.*

Later that day, it was Bernard's turn to play with the Lego. The teacher gently explained to him that in school all children had to share and take their turn. Bernard repeated this tantrum, but with diminishing frequency as the weeks went by, until one day he announced, 'You know, teacher, I only have tantrums at home now'. When his parents heard this, they enlisted the support of the teacher to help Bernard realise that tantrums do not work at home either.

4 Should I Worry about Academic Ability?

Academic ability is a primary concern for parents and many ask when and if they should start teaching their children to read, write and do their sums. Should they start before they go to school?

This chapter examines this concern and helps parents to see that almost from the moment a child opens their eyes, they have started to develop the basic observational skills that will allow them to later read, make shapes, add and subtract, and explore their world in so many other ways.

As a baby looks around their new world, they will first observe the faces of the people who nurture them. They will observe the different colours, shapes, sizes and textures in their surroundings. They will look intently at the red wooden block, turn it several times, taste it, look again, feel its corners and flat surfaces, and all the time their observation skills are being sharpened. While playing on the floor with their toys they will learn to differentiate between toys that are soft or hard, toys that roll or stack, toys that have corners or are round and smooth, and all the other qualities that attach to their playthings. Of course, the young child is not consciously saying, 'Oh! That teddy is soft and smooth', or 'That car is hard', but through the play process, whether on their own, with the adults in their life or with their peers, your child is learning and putting in place the building blocks for reading, writing and arithmetic.

Beginning the Reading Process

Your child's language development, from the gurgle to the single word to the broken sentence and, finally, to the simple sentence structure, is a vital preparation for reading progress and can be developed by:

- Taking time to talk with your child as they observe the world around them. This will familiarise them with the rhythm of speech and build their vocabulary.

- Teaching your child simple nursery rhymes. This is great fun and is a great learning tool. As reading is mostly about recognising similar, written, individual sounds and rhymes, the more highly developed your child's ear is to these sounds and rhymes the better. As your child laughs and giggles through 'Humpty Dumpty sat on the wall, Humpty Dumpty had a great fall', he is learning that 'wall' and 'fall' rhyme, without you having to draw attention to it.

Introducing Books

When should you introduce books to your child? Early, early, early! Children take a great interest in pictures long before they realise that the written word means something. The young child will babble their way through the pictures in a book, pointing out the most obscure object for special attention. Snuggling up to an adult and listening to a story is not only a wonderful foundation for reading, but can also be an opportunity for the child to confide in the adult if something is bothering them. In the intimacy of story time, a child feels secure and loved. All these positive feelings will foster a desire to read. Story time should be a joy for your child.

Good language development and an interest in and love of books are the best foundation you can give your child for reading. Send your child into school with these skills and reading will nearly always be a smooth and exciting journey. Each school has its own reading programme and you will be guided through this process by the teacher. Read to your child on a daily basis and do not stop reading to them when they start school or when they can read fluently. Continue to have story time and treat it as a golden moment of intimacy between adult and child.

Lead by Example

Another vital preparation for reading comes from observing how the adults in their world treat the written word:

- How often does a child see the adults read a book, paper or magazine?
- Do the adults take an obvious delight and pleasure in the written word?
- Is the child surrounded mostly by the constant flickering of the TV or other modern technology? It is important to be selective in the amount of television viewing, as constant noise stresses children, revs them up physically and lowers their concentration.

Do not Over-Encourage

Some children will show an interest in the written word before they start school and will often point to words and say, 'What's that?' Of course, the adult should tell the child, but not try to turn the child's enthusiastic questioning into more of a joy for them than it is for the child. Some parents boast to everyone who comes into that home, 'Look! Listen to Joe! He's only three and he can read!' On that particular day, maybe Joe is in a bad mood or doesn't want to perform and so lets his parents down, even after much prompting and encouragement. If the parent shows annoyance or disappointment, it can change Joe's attitude to reading. When the mechanics of reading become more important than the joy and love of reading, it is time to take a step back and slow down your own desire to have Joe reading early. Let reading be a natural development for your child, full of exploration and fun, and let books be their friend. A child who loves books is seldom lonely or bored.

Use the Library

Let us not forget that in this age of technology, children and adults have a wonderful facility available to them in their local library. Parents sometimes have difficulty in selecting a suitable book for their child and may be unaware of the wealth of knowledge and guidance available to them from the librarian. As you accumulate more books at home, you may feel that you have no need to go to the library, but a trip to the library is a joy and a pleasure for any child.

Be Patient and Encourage Effort

As your child struggles through the initial stages of reading, they will make many mistakes. They may read 'house' as 'horse' or 'witch' as 'which'. Encourage rather than correct every effort they make and soon they will be self-correcting to make sense of the story that they are reading. 'I can read that! I can read that!' they will announce proudly, until one day they will take their new skill for granted and you will notice them just relaxing and enjoying a book or comic.

Writing

Teachers do not expect children to be able to write when they come to school. It is far more important that small children have had plenty of opportunity to build up the control in their little hands. This will help them when they start to write.

Practical Tips

- The assembling and pulling apart of construction toys from a very early age will develop dexterity – Lego, Mobilo, Playmobil, interconnecting blocks etc.
- Playing with dolls – dressing and undressing them, brushing their hair, washing them etc.
- Manipulating pliable materials such as playdough, plasticine and any leftover pastry at baking time.
- Outdoor play – climbing, swinging, water and sand play, and other playground equipment.
- From a very young age, children are attracted to scribbling, so have plenty of thick crayons and paper at hand and allow them the freedom to explore this

medium. Try not to impose any structure on their scribbling at this point, as all that is needed right now is to strengthen their hand control. Over time, they will develop more control themselves and enjoy colouring.

- Simple colouring books are useful. Encourage children to stay inside the lines and praise them for every effort. As their hands develop, so will the quality of the colouring.
- A painting easel or sheets of newspaper on the floor or on the table provide children the opportunity to use paint and brushes.
- Using old magazines and catalogues to tear and stick or to cut and stick. Always use a child's safety scissors.

As children mature they may take an interest in the written word. Do not teach them how to write formally, as each school has its own system of teaching letter formation. Encourage every effort that they make, but do not worry if they are not showing a huge interest in writing before they start school. When the teacher begins to teach formal writing, children with well-developed hands will learn to write with ease.

Mathematical language will develop, as children are surrounded by colour, shape, different sized objects and a large variety of stimulating materials. When playing with their toys, they will be constantly:

- Classifying: putting soldiers, teddy bears or similar toys in groups.
- Matching: grouping objects by colour or size.

- Comparing: children are aware when a friend's toy is bigger or stronger than theirs.
- Ordering: building towers according to the size of blocks, tubs or boxes.

Toys and opportunity to play will help to develop the above skills without too much input from an adult.

Numerical language needs a more conscious effort on behalf of the adults in the child's life. It is advisable to introduce numbers informally:

- Shopping: occasionally use numbers when letting children help you in the supermarket, for example: 'Let's get four yoghurts', 'We need two boxes of Cornflakes' and so on.
- Mealtimes: allow children to help you count out cutlery for everybody.
- Count steps on the stairs: it will help to familiarise children with the language of counting.
- Tidying: instead of saying, 'Pick up your toys', perhaps you could say, 'Pick up the two books, the three dolls ...'
- Birthdays: blowing out three or four candles etc.

There will be many more opportunities to introduce numerical language informally as children develop. At this stage, children do not need to understand numbers – they just need to be familiar with the language. When they go to school, it will then be easier for them to go forward with their own learning. This should never become a conscious teaching exercise or a burden to small children.

Susan

By the time Susan was three years old, her parents were aware that she was a bright, confident girl. She thrived in pre-school and had wonderful language, loved stories, drawing and painting. Susan could not wait to start big school. Her parents decided that it would give her a head start if they taught her to write her numbers. Numbers one, four and seven were no problem, but when it came to writing the numbers two, three, five and eight, Susan became very frustrated. The more her parents corrected her efforts, the more tense she became. Before long, Susan associated paper and pencil with hard work.

In Junior School, her attitude to pencil and paper did not change. The teacher had a word with Susan's parents and they realised that perhaps they had introduced the written number too early. Rather than having a head start, Susan took a long time to become comfortable and relaxed using a pencil and paper.

Let the desire to write numbers come from children. They often like to copy older brothers and sisters. Praise their efforts, but do not over-correct them. Do not be surprised if young children switch from writing numbers to drawing a volcano on the same page – to them they are all just pictures!

The best head start to give children is to allow them to play thoroughly, letting their little hands develop naturally before introducing structured work.

5 What if my Child doesn't Make Friends?

From an early age, some children make friends very quickly, while others are more cautious. Making friends is a natural process and, given time, most children will form friendships. Parents realise the importance of good friends and are delighted when their child socialises easily. Of course there are children who are shy and do not make friends easily. This can be a worry for some parents, who fear that their son or daughter will feel lonely or isolated when they venture out from the safety of the home and neighbourhood they know and feel comfortable in. While it is true that moving beyond the comfort zone carries the risk of rejection, it is also true that it represents the beginning of an adventure which enhances the child's ability to relate to new people, to respect the rights and needs of others, to practise compromise and to begin the process of forming new friendships that may last a lifetime.

Every classroom has a mix of personalities, from the quiet, gentle child to the boisterous, assertive one. This chapter explores how to promote the kind of behaviour that not only facilitates learning but also allows harmony and friendship to blossom between the different personalities.

Good Manners

The seeds of friendship grow through good manners. When a child comes to school with basic good manners, they find it much easier to negotiate with their peers and to communicate with the teacher. In our experience, well-mannered children are the most popular in any group. The child who grabs, pushes and demands their own way may find themselves very quickly excluded from the best games. The lively, boisterous child may be very popular at first, but if they turn out to be rude and ill mannered, that popularity often wanes. However, if their personality is backed up by good manners, they will continue to be well liked. Good manners will help the quiet, introverted child to integrate more easily: for example, 'Can I be in your game, please?' has a much better chance of success than, 'I want to play that game'.

When explaining to children what we mean by good manners, it is good to point out that good manners mean:

- Saying 'Please' and 'Thank you'.
- Recognising that someone has been kind or has done something for you.
- Accepting or refusing something gracefully when a choice is offered: for example, saying, 'Yes please' or 'No thank you', rather than, 'I don't want it'.
- Recognising the effort someone makes in selecting a gift for you, even if you do not like it. (The look of sadness on a child's face when their gift is rejected is heartbreaking!)
- Apologising when you have done something naughty.
- Respecting others' choices, being patient and waiting your turn.

- Knowing how to behave at the table. Children eat in a group at school, so encourage them to have good table manners, such as avoiding speaking with a mouthful of food and refraining from slurping their drink.

We firmly believe that adults should start a campaign of commenting favourably on good behaviour in children when they see it. The next time you are in a restaurant, church or on public transport and you notice well-behaved children, showing consideration for others, compliment the child and the parents. We should recognise and encourage good manners in children, rather than criticise unruly behaviour. Never underestimate the value and impact that good manners have on others.

Avoid Teasing

Children enjoy banter and jesting, but when it gets too personal it hurts. For a class to run smoothly, children also need to learn not to tease but to try to be kind, gentle and patient, and to understand differences in each other. The dictionary defines teasing as 'to annoy someone playfully, especially by ridicule'. Children are often shocked if their little friend gets upset and begins to cry. When they are reprimanded, they always say, 'But I was only joking'. We tell them that a joke is only funny when the other person is laughing too.

Most children come to school with many of the skills and attributes of good manners that we have outlined. However, for others it can be quite a painful experience to discover that other children have rights too, as Martin's story demonstrates.

Martin

Martin was a boisterous, assertive little boy. At home, Mum and Dad encouraged the other children to humour him. 'I want my dinner first! I want my dinner first!' he would shout. Martin was pacified and was always served first. At story time, Martin would demand that his choice of story be read first. It did not matter to him what the other children wanted. 'Read this one, Dad!' he would plead. Dad always gave in, as he did not want Martin upset at bedtime. Martin was equally assertive with his playmates, dictating the course of every game. 'Maybe he's going to be a leader,' Dad said comfortingly to Mum.

So, off to school Martin went. 'I want to paint now!', 'I want the train jigsaw!', 'I want to sit next to James!', 'I want to be the leader!' said

Martin, and he could not understand why the teacher chose other children for these activities.

He complained bitterly at home. 'Don't worry, pet,' said Mum. 'I'll talk to the teacher and we'll sort it out.' It did not take Mum and Dad long to realise that Martin got his own way far too much at home. He was confused and disappointed when his strategies for getting his own way did not work at school. There, all the children had equal rights. It was the teacher's duty to ensure that the quiet child's rights were not infringed.

Between Mum, Dad and teacher, it was decided that Martin would be encouraged and taught, in a very gentle but firm way, that all the children in his class had the same rights as he had. He would have to wait his turn to paint, wait for the train jigsaw and wait his turn to be the leader. Most importantly, James was already sitting beside Adam, with whom he got on very well, so it was not possible for Martin to sit there right now.

At home, his parents started listening to the other children's requests and needs. They often put them first, even if it resulted in some appalling outbursts of frustration from Martin. Before the end of Martin's first year in school, while still being boisterous and assertive, he had learned that taking turns and respecting other children's rights were part of all aspects of his life and not just school life.

How many Friends do our Children Need?

Some children like to be in the middle of everything, organising all of the games. They like to have lots of friends and are happiest when they are surrounded by people. Other children are quieter by nature and are equally happy with one or two friends playing in a small group.

Allow your child to develop their own level of friendships. Do not be anxious if they are not extroverts, as being quiet is a virtue, not a fault.

The Things that Children Say

All parents want their children to be well liked, well behaved and popular with their peers. However, sometimes the things that children say can give parents the impression that the opposite is the case.

Nobody will play with me

This is a common complaint and is usually the result of children naturally moving from group to group in the playground, depending on the games being played. Occasionally, a child may have difficulty joining a game already in progress. Instead of asking if they may take part, they wait to be invited. They watch the children having fun and feel rejected. The other children are oblivious to their distress. When they announce at home, 'Nobody wants to play with me in the playground', they mean it and they are genuinely upset. A word with the teacher usually sorts this out.

I never get a turn at...

Children hate waiting. They are especially impatient when waiting for their favourite game or book. An infant classroom is like a little factory, with everything rotating throughout the week. Children get to use all of the equipment in the classroom, but not on the one day. When the complaint is made, 'I never get a turn at...', be sympathetic and assure the child that their turn will come. What the child means is, 'I want it now and I don't like waiting'. It will help your child in school if they are expected to wait their turn at home. Praise them when they show signs of patience. Children thrive on praise.

He made me do it
When a child starts school, their sense of responsibility is still in the developmental stage. If they misbehave and are challenged, their response will often be, 'He made me do it'.

Children really believe that they are good and that another child made them do the naughty act. It is a great statement of self-preservation. The blame is moved, so now everything should be forgiven or forgotten. It takes time, patience and understanding to help the young child realise that they alone are responsible for their behaviour. Sometimes, a child may even create an imaginary 'naughty friend' who is to blame for every misdemeanour. Learning to take responsibility comes with maturity and good training. Teacher and parents working together will help your child to set their own standards.

He was doing it too
Children love comrades in crime. When the offence is shared between two or three children, they really do believe that a problem shared is a problem halved. So, when a teacher asks, 'Why were you flicking paint?' the answer invariably is, 'He was

doing it too'. We have all used this response, so we understand how the small child feels. Of course, they are a lot less vulnerable if their little friend is standing beside them. It is important that, as they mature, they realise that they alone are responsible for their actions. Parents and teachers need to guide the child gently in this direction. Occasionally, a child will deny outright their involvement in the misbehaviour. They are too young to understand the importance of truthfulness. A truthful child is rarely accused in the wrong, as their reputation for owning up protects them. They are also more popular with their peers if they do not blame them.

We can encourage our children to be truthful by:

- Removing the element of fear.
- Accepting that your child is human and will often make little mistakes.
- Keeping the punishment in proportion to the misdemeanour.
- Ensuring that the adult in charge deals with the incident as soon as possible, avoids delayed punishments and does not refer to it again. Children need forgiveness in order to thrive.

Everybody is getting...
This is a very old line. We know, because we often used it ourselves: 'Everybody is getting one except me.' Most parents have enough sense to see it for what it is – a tug at the guilt strings. Try not to be influenced or blackmailed by what other parents are giving to their children.

Everybody is going…

The first year in school, when a child says, 'Everybody is going', it usually means a birthday party. Children talk a lot about their parties, especially about who will and will not be invited. The list of guests changes all the time. When a child comes home from school and announces that everybody is going to the latest movie, the circus, the pantomime, ice-skating, a puppet show, a football match or indeed a birthday party, just remember that 'everybody' can mean as few as four or five children, as Anna's story proves.

Anna

Sophie, Anna's classmate, was going to be five soon. Her Mum said that she could invite eight girls from school to her party. Mum did not know the children, so she let Sophie decide on the guest list. Sophie changed her mind several times before the final decision was made. To Anna, it looked like she was the only one not being invited. 'Have you got an invitation for me?' she asked. 'No,' answered Sophie, 'you can't come.' Poor Anna was devastated to think that the whole class was going to the party and that she would be home alone. When Anna's parents enquired discreetly, they were relieved to discover that Anna was one of twenty other children who were not invited to Sophie's party. Anna felt much better when this was explained to her.

6 Could my Child be Bullied?

It can be difficult for the young child to differentiate between bullying and rough play. Having acknowledged this, it is also important to recognise that bullying happens in all sections of society and amongst all age groups. Therefore, it is something that should be taken seriously by parents who should know what to do if they suspect that their child is a victim of bullying at school. Today, all schools have policies in place to address the problem of bullying and if they haven't already been provided with the procedure, parents should ask to see the policy that their chosen school has in place should such a circumstance arise.

In this chapter we will look at a case of rough play, examine the tell-tale signs of bullying and suggest ways to deal with it if you find that your child has been a victim of bullying. We will also look at the needs of the child who has engaged in bullying and suggest ways to help the child change their behaviour.

What is Rough Play?

A strong personality does not denote a bully. Some children are boisterous by nature and may appear rough to other children. Sometimes they are having so much fun that they are not taking the quieter child's needs into consideration. They are quick to apologise when they realise that they have upset somebody.

This is what happened when Simon and Andrew were playing in the school playground.

Simon

When the children settle in school, they begin to form friendships and these friendships are rather fluid in the playground. Children tend to move from one group to another, depending on the game being played and on their own mood on the day. So it was with Andrew and Simon. They formed a friendship in the first week and gravitated towards each other most days in the playground. Their favourite game was called 'Sharks'. Lots of other children joined in this exciting game. One boy was chosen as the shark. The others had to escape into the ocean before the shark captured them. Andrew, who was a strong boy, was often chosen to be the shark. During the capturing process, amid hoots of laughter, shouts of 'You can't catch me! You can't catch me!' Simon was sometimes captured. In the rough and tumble that occasionally followed, Simon got the odd scratch. He was having such fun that these little scratches did not bother him. Mum saw things differently. Andrew's name was mentioned a little too often when the scratches were remarked upon. She discussed it with Dad and they both decided that Simon was being bullied by Andrew. They met with Simon's teacher, and it was a huge relief to them that this was not so.

What is Bullying?

Bullying is persistent verbal, physical or emotional ill-treatment.

- Examples of verbal bullying: repeated negative remarks about a child's appearance, home, family or ability.
- Examples of physical bullying: repeated hitting, pushing, kicking, pinching, pulling hair and so on.
- Examples of emotional bullying: causing a child to be isolated from a group, laughing at their mistakes or mishaps, telling them in front of others that they will not be invited to a party and so on.

The Bully and the Victim

In children, bullying is frequently related to low levels of self-esteem in the bully and also in the victim. The bully may need to find someone to torment and victimise to validate themselves. Often, because of the victim's low self-esteem they have not developed the necessary skills to identify the problem early enough and are unable to stand up to the bully. They may be reluctant to seek help for fear of retaliation.

Good self-esteem is crucial to developing a well-rounded child who is not just concerned about their own well-bring but is equally aware of the needs of those around them. It will help them to cope with life in a more positive way.

What should I do if I Think my Child is being Bullied?

All schools have an anti-bullying policy. Teachers are aware of how important it is to be vigilant and alert to the possibility of bullying between children. School policies may vary slightly but they all have the well-being of the child as a priority.

When a parent suspects that a child is being bullied, it is best to handle it sooner rather than later. Discuss the problem with the child. Talk to the class teacher, who will implement the school policy and attempt to sort out the problem to everybody's satisfaction. It is important to make children aware that bulling is unacceptable and that disclosing it is the right thing to do.

The school policy makes children aware that:

- Bullying is unacceptable.
- Informing a teacher is necessary and important.
- A record will be kept.
- The incident will be investigated.
- A solution will be sought that may involve both sets of parents.

The child who feels bullied needs to:

- Feel confident that bullies will not be tolerated.
- Be enabled to say 'No' in a loud, clear voice, as bullies hate negative attention.
- Be able to tell someone they can trust.
- Realise that by ignoring the initial verbal taunts of a bully, they may stop, as bullies hate being ignored.

What should I do if I Think my Child is Bullying other Children?

It is important to observe our children at play. Personalities come to the fore when children are with their peers. If your child is more assertive than you are comfortable with, if they insist on their choice of game being played every time, if they exclude other children who do not agree with them and if they are unnecessarily rough, they may have a problem with bullying.

The bully also needs guidance and understanding to enable them to change their behaviour.

- Most bullies suffer from low self-esteem.
- Bullies often do to others what has been done to them.
- Bullies need help to realise that:
  - drawing attention to perceived imperfections is hurtful;
  - isolating and undermining other children is unacceptable;
  - children can be hurt inside as well as outside – emotionally as well as physical.

Be aware that jealousy is one of the main causes of bullying.

Ben

Ben was a popular little boy in the playground and lots of games revolved around him. His popularity irked Fintan, so he set about excluding Ben from the group. This was done in a subtle way. The other boys were unaware of what was happening. It began with gentle, negative suggestions. Fintan whispered to the other children: 'Ben thinks that he is always the boss', 'Ben's game is a stupid game', 'Ben is wearing girls' runners', 'Don't ask Ben to your party', 'Ben said that you were a baby'. Bit by bit, Ben was elbowed out of the group.

The teacher noticed that Ben had changed from a happy, outgoing boy to a much quieter, less confident child. During this time, Fintan never touched Ben or showed any physical aggression towards him. It was difficult for Ben to complain at home, as he had no visible marks. But the torment, undermining and humiliation that Ben suffered, if left unchecked, would have had serious consequences for him. The teacher sent for Ben's parents and they, too, were perplexed about the changes in Ben. They eliminated home and the classroom as the cause of his unhappiness.

Circle time exposed the problem, as one little boy blurted out, 'We can't play with Ben in the playground anymore because Fintan won't let us'. The teacher now knew that Ben was being bullied and that both Fintan and Ben needed help. The teacher and Fintan's parents worked closely together. They explained to him that his unkind words hurt deeply. To help him develop his self-esteem, the teacher gave him a few little responsibilities. His parents monitored his behaviour at home more closely, watching out for signs of him bullying friends who came to play. They removed him from his friends when bullying occurred.

Bullying is not cured overnight but, with parents and teachers working together, the young child leans to communicate in a kinder way.

Ben was made aware that he was not responsible for Fintan's behaviour. The teacher spoke to the class and encouraged them to not only be aware of their own needs, but also the needs of others. Ben was given lots of praise and encouragement to restore his confidence. Now that the problem had been identified and dealt with, it did not take Ben long to regain his popularity.

The teacher advised Ben's parents to encourage him to be more assertive. When feeling bullied, he should look the other boy directly in the face and say in a loud, clear voice — 'Stop doing that! I don't like it!' This will attract the teacher's attention, and bullies hate the spotlight.

7 How Important is Diet?

What your child eats for lunch in school will influence their concentration for the rest of the school day. That is why most schools promote and encourage healthy food in the lunchbox. Occasionally, parents will tell us that children will not eat certain foods. They insist that they do not like bread, cheese, ham, chicken, rice cakes, carrots, celery, apples, oranges, bananas, yoghurts, milk and other healthy options.

When the lunch is being prepared on that first morning, some parents may not want to add to the excitement and stress by insisting on a healthy lunch. It is easier to give the child what they ask for, which may be crackers, biscuits, bars, crisps and highly coloured sweet juices. Once this habit is established, it is very difficult to change it.

From our experience, a child's diet and nutrition has a significant effect on their concentration and behaviour. We have noticed that when some children come to school, they are fidgety, slightly agitated and restless. They can sometimes be silly and interrupt quite a lot. It is difficult for them to maintain concentration and to settle down to a task. Their little bodies are in constant motion, hopping up and down, feet all over the place, interfering with other children's belongings. When we observe the contents of their lunch boxes over a few weeks, we suspect that their behaviour may be influenced by diet.

In this chapter we will look at why diet is important and suggest ways of maintaining a healthy diet that will enhance your child's attitude to food and improve their capacity for concentration.

How do I Make my Child Eat Healthy Food?

Encourage healthy eating from an early age. Children are influenced by the adults in their lives. It is important to eat at least one meal a day together at the table. This will encourage them to eat what you eat and to enjoy food. Limit the amount of junk food in the cupboards: if it is not there, they cannot eat it. It is very useful to have a good book on nutrition as a guide to healthy eating.

What Kind of Foods are Better?

Drinks are important, but read the labels carefully and be aware that too many additives can be harmful to children. Make treats as healthy as possible – a piece of chocolate, home-made buns or biscuits. Avoid highly sugared and highly salted foods for the young child.

Be Practical

- Choose a lunchbox that your child can manage on their own.
- Ensure that they can open all fruit and packaging to avoid distress.
- Give small portions and make the contents of the lunchbox attractive.

Healthy Lunchbox Options

- Brown bread or pitta bread sandwich – chicken, tuna, cheese.
- Left-over rice or pasta salad.
- Some vegetables – carrot, cucumber or pepper sticks.
- Piece of cheese.
- Fruit – banana, apple, raisins, grapes.

- Yoghurt or milk drink.
- Healthy drink – water or milk.

Let us have a look at what happens to Harry when he eats the unhealthy contents of his lunchbox.

Harry

For lunch today, Harry had crackers with chocolate spread, a chocolate bar and a sweet drink. He had already had a very restless morning in school, had difficulty concentrating and was constantly distracting both teacher and boys with his giddy behaviour. After lunch, things got worse. Harry was unable to finish any tasks and could not sit still when the teacher was reading his favourite story. Harry got upset when the teacher corrected him on a few occasions as he loved school and really was a very good child. The teacher suspected that Harry's diet was contributing to his restless behaviour. She spoke to his parents and discovered that Harry was a poor eater and finicky about his food. They were delighted that he was eating anything at all.

At first they found it difficult to accept that Harry's diet was contributing to his hyperactivity, but were prepared to try healthier options. The transition from unhealthy to healthy food was not easy. Harry put up many a battle, but with perseverance and encouragement from family and teacher, he began to enjoy his new diet. Within a short time, the teacher noticed a huge improvement in Harry's behaviour and his parents were overjoyed.

8 Can I Help my Child to Handle Change?

Children always look to their parents for confirmation that life is going well. By the time a child reaches school-going age, they could do a thesis on their parents' facial expressions. So even when we try to shield our children from some family upset, more often than not the child will sense that something is not right just by looking at our faces. This may affect the child's behaviour in school: a once outgoing child may become withdrawn, anxious or disruptive; the quiet child may be emotional and weepy.

There will be times when sharing some information with the child may be possible: for example, when Granny is unwell. However, a child may need to be shielded from other problems. Until you are ready to talk to your child about the problem, be very careful about what they may overhear.

During a time of crisis or change in the home, it is important that the teacher is made aware that all is not well. The teacher will then be very sympathetic to any changes in the child's behaviour and will be a huge support to them.

Just as children pick up when we are upset or sad, they also pick up when we are happy or excited. In our experience, the two things that excite a small child most are the arrival of a new baby and moving house. In this chapter we will examine ways of managing both events for the benefit of the whole family.

The New Baby

Children get very excited when they are told that they are getting a new baby. They cannot wait to declare their great news to the teacher and to everybody who will listen. Small children have no concept of time and expect the new baby to arrive fairly soon after being told. Six or seven months seems forever to them. If children know too far in advance, it may confuse them, especially if another child in the class gets their new baby first. We have often heard small children exclaim, 'My Mum is getting a baby but it's taking a long, long time!' If all is going well, perhaps the second half of the pregnancy is time enough to inform the young child. However, children worry, so if Mum is ill during the early weeks of the pregnancy, it is best to tell them that Mum is getting a new baby and to reassure them that everything will be alright.

We have found that the following guidelines are useful when a family has had, or is anticipating, a new arrival:

- Collect the child from school on time, as they will be more emotional right now with the new baby in the house.

- Try to arrange the baby's nap soon after the older child comes home from school. Let that be their special time.
- When family and friends call to admire the new baby, encourage them to admire the older child too.
- Some young children may feel upset when they see Mum walking away from the classroom door with the new baby in her arms. The child is usually happier to see the baby in the pram or buggy.
- Let the child introduce the new baby to their teacher. It will help them to be proud of their new brother or sister.

As the new baby gets older and more interesting, the young child will develop a close bond with them and no longer see them as an intruder.

A new baby is a joy and a blessing for any family. However, for the child who has had the undivided attention of both parents it can be a shock, as Karen's story exemplifies. Allow the child time to develop their own relationship with the baby and they will have a friend for life.

Karen

'You are so lucky, Karen, you'll be getting a new baby soon. You'll have great fun with the baby and you'll be able to help Mum.' Karen was delighted. As the day drew near, Karen listened to Mum's tummy and could hear the heartbeat. She even felt the

baby kick a few times. At last, Mum went into hospital. There was great excitement when baby Peter was born. Karen could not wait for Peter to come home and, when he did, she danced up and down with joy.

Even though Karen could not see it herself, everyone remarked on how beautiful Peter was. All she knew was that Peter was not much fun. He spent most of the day sleeping, feeding or up in Mum's arms – those very arms that were meant for her.

Karen loved helping Mum care for Peter, especially as Mum was tired and needed lots of rest. Even though Karen was looking forward to returning to school, when the day arrived, something was different. When they arrived at the school, Mum lifted Peter out of his car seat and held him in her arms. As Mum bent down to kiss Karen goodbye, Peter was between them. Karen went in to school a little sadder that morning, knowing that Peter would be up in Mum's arms all day while she was at school. And as far as she was concerned, she was right. Wasn't he up in Mum's arms every day when she collected Karen from school? Karen appeared a little distracted in school and was very easily upset. The teacher asked her what the matter was, and Karen immediately burst out, 'I was just thinking about my Mum. We have a new baby, you know, and my Mum has lots of work to do'. The teacher realised that the new baby was confusing Karen's emotions. When the teacher spoke to Mum, she agreed that Karen's behaviour had also changed at home since the baby's arrival.

Mum made a little bit of extra time for Karen. Instead of using Peter's nap time to catch up on household chores, she gave that time to Karen for the first few weeks. She sat with her, read to her and gently and kindly reassured her. When Peter started to smile and respond to Karen, she no longer felt threatened by him and started to enjoy her role as his big sister.

Moving House

What makes the young child secure in their own home? It is not any one thing, but a combination of many things. The people that they love most in the world live there. They know every corner, every item of furniture and, most importantly, where all of their toys and books are stored. Their house has a special smell, which gives them a warm feeling of safety and security when they come in the door.

When a child has moved house, it is a time for parents to be extra patient and understanding. The child misses that familiar smell, that special corner for everything and, most importantly, their friends. There can be a conflict of feelings, excitement and anticipation on the one hand, and a feeling of loss and loneliness on the other. They may fluctuate between loving everything about their new life and longing to return to their old, familiar house.

When a change of house means a change of school, a child has a lot more adjusting to do. In such circumstances it is important to:

- Tell the child as much as you can about their new school and new teacher. Introduce them to the teacher before their starting date, if possible.

- Do not rush them into making new friends, as they will do this when they are ready.
- Be confident that your child will be inviting friends to play within a short time.
- Reading a story book about moving house will give them an idea of what is happening – encourage them to ask questions.
- Keep in regular contact with the teacher to ensure that the child is settling in.

It may also help your child if you:

- Introduce yourself and your family to your immediate neighbours by calling on them when you settle in. It will be wonderful if they have children of a similar age to yours.
- Find out where the nearest children's playground is located. It is a good place to meet other parents and young children.
- When your child starts school, some names will be mentioned more often than others. Arrange with their parents for these new friends to come to play.
- Take the children for walks around your neighbourhood. It will help you to get to know the people in your area.
- Encourage children who live near you to play in your home and garden. Have your home child friendly.

Richard's story is typical of the conflicting emotions that occur at a time of change.

Richard

Richard loved his own house more than any other house. So when Mum and Dad announced that they were moving, Richard was a little sad. It did not take him long to brighten up when his parents explained to him that the new house would be bigger, nearer to Granny and that all of his books and toys would be going to live there too. By the time the day of the big move arrived, Richard was very excited as he waved goodbye to his friends. He knew that he was going to love his new house and his new school, because Mum and Dad had told him so.

When they arrived at the new house, Richard rushed out of the car to check out his new surroundings. The house was bigger, Mum and Dad were right about that, and the garden was beautiful. Richard was busy over the next few days, unpacking his belongings and finding special places for his books and toys.

Later that week, his parents noticed that he was quieter than usual and very easily upset. During story time that evening, Richard said, 'I wish that my friends lived here too. I have no one to play with'. Dad comforted him, knowing that it would take Richard time to find his feet, feel comfortable in his new home, make new friends and settle into a new school.

9 Is Free Time Wasted Time?

If it is Monday, it must be tennis; Tuesday, art; Wednesday, dancing; Thursday, swimming; Friday, music; Saturday and Sunday are for sport, and then we start all over again on Monday. The result is that Mum and Dad are worn out, and the child is exhausted too!

Ask yourself – how do you feel at the end of your working day? How often do you feel like attending a class that requires concentration? How often do you feel like going straight to the gym? How often do you feel like socialising with new people? Children may appear to have energy to spare at all times but, like adults, it is important to build in time to allow them to switch off and relax. This chapter shows the importance of allowing children to have relaxation time, giving them time to daydream, time to let their imagination entertain them or simply to play.

Play is Hard Work

School is a wonderful place for children today. It is full of all kinds of stimulating experiences that challenge and develop your child. Parents are often surprised at how tired children are at the end of play. But remember that play is like work to the young child. Children are both physically and emotionally tired by the time the school day is over, which is why they are sometimes grumpy on the way home. This does not mean your child did not enjoy their day, simply that they are only five and need a rest.

After-School Activities are still Important

You may ask – are all activities after school more of a burden than a pleasure for your child? Of course not, but every waking moment does not need to be crammed and busy. It is by observing our fellow humans, as well as interacting with them, that we learn. While physical activity and interaction with their peers are hugely important to the overall development of our children, in the modern world, the interaction element has been over-emphasised. Parents feel guilty if a child uses the word 'bored'. It triggers the failure button in them. They feel responsible and rush to fill the void with something. The modern parent is uneasy with the inactive child. They assume that they are either lazy or uninterested and that both conditions need to be cured. Never assume that a child who is quiet is bored. Their imagination is like a computer and will never fail to entertain them.

We should always allow our children time and space to stand and stare, and so it is worth considering the following points:

- Try not to fill every moment of your child's life with physical activity.
- Allow time and space for a child's imagination to work.
- Your child does not need friends playing with them at all times. Sometimes, children like to play on their own.
- When you do not react to the phrase 'I'm bored', the child will soon find something to do.
- Try not to have too many extracurricular activities that are success-driven. Allow time for you and your child to enjoy each other's company: perhaps a visit to the library, a walk in the park, a child's day out at an art gallery or museum, or sitting on the sofa together reading a story.
- Encourage your child to appreciate simple things – watching a bird feeding in the garden, a worm wriggling on the footpath, raindrops trickling down the windowpane or clouds drifting by.

Sarah's story illustrates the importance of allowing children to daydream.

Sarah

Sarah was a lovely child, who played very well with the other children. She also liked playing on her own. Her art work was most imaginative and full of colour and life. One day, the teacher noticed that Sarah was sitting alone, while the other children played a game. The teacher called Sarah to do her supervised table work. Sarah did not respond. The teacher called her again. Still no response. The teacher went over to Sarah, gently touched her on the shoulder and said, 'Sarah, it is your turn to come to the table, please'. Sarah looked up, blinked a few times and burst out crying. This took the teacher by surprise, as Sarah normally loved table work. 'What is the matter?' asked the teacher. 'I was just going to the ball, and now I can't,' cried Sarah. The teacher understood immediately and tried to comfort Sarah, saying, 'The table work won't take long, and you can go to the ball later'. 'No, I can't,' sobbed Sarah, 'because now you vanished it!' Sarah was not sitting there doing nothing. She was creating her own moments of wonder, magic and entertainment in her head.

Free Play

Social skills are best developed in the young child under the watchful eye of an adult. Children love inviting their friends to play in their own homes. Sometimes parents may feel that they have a responsibility to entertain the young visitors.

Naturally the adults want the children to go away saying, 'We had a great time at Barry's house'. But the young child needs very little to entertain them. How often has a small child shown much more interest in the box than the expensive toy inside?

Construction toys such a Lego, blocks, Playmobil or Mobilo will develop a child's hand skills, imagination and co-operative play. Toys such as cars, soldiers, dolls and all their accessories keep children happily occupied for hours.

Modern technology plays a very significant part in young children's lives. As it is so easily accessible, it is important that an adult decides what is suitable viewing for children. No doubt, you will be told that everyone in the class is allowed to watch a certain programme, but you decide what is best for your child.

Children become computer literate at a very early age and this is wonderful. Be aware that computer games and Playstations may become addictive. Limit the time they spend on them. It is best for children to have lots of free time to play with other children and so develop their social and emotional skills.

Lots of children love sport, and from a very young age many have their own sporting heroes who they want to emulate. All schools encourage and promote physical education and every child is given the opportunity to develop their own potential. It is important to nurture any sporting talent a child may have. It is also important that a child has fun and enjoys developing that ability. Gentle encouragement is healthy, but over-enthusiastic pressure may become a burden to the small child. The majority of our children are happy to be involved in sport and given the opportunity will soon find their own level. The objective of sport is to develop healthy bodies, healthy minds and to have lots of fun.

Conclusion: Enjoy Your Child!

We have given you many tips in these pages to help you help your child get the most from the exciting days of their early school-going years. But the most important piece of advice we can give to you is to enjoy your child. Your child is unique, so let them be just that. Nurture and develop the talents and abilities they have by praising and encouraging little achievements. Notice the positive as much as possible. As they make their journey through school, try not to compare them with other children. Let them be the best that they can be at art, writing, reading, sport and the wide variety of subjects in the school curriculum. Encourage them in their friendships. Ensure that there is time for family outings, free play, lounging about and relaxing and just having fun.

Learn to Edit

There is plenty of advice out there. When listening to other parents and to extended family, edit a lot of what you hear. It is human nature to embellish our children's successes and to omit talking about their little hiccups. Many of us see our children through rose-tinted glasses.

Have Fun

Make time and space for the personal enjoyment of your own life. Your child will then learn from observing you that life does not have to be serious all the time. The best gift that you can give to your child is to be the most loving and caring parent that you can be. Minimise problems, as with loving care they will sort themselves out.

Children are wonderful. Enjoy and appreciate each phase of their development. Childhood is the foundation of our journey through life and therefore it is a very precious time.

NMCCexp

We hope you enjoy this book. Please return or renew it by the due date.

You can renew it at www.norfolk.gov.uk/libraries or by using our free library app.

Otherwise you can phone 0344 800 8020 - please have your library card and PIN ready.

You can sign up for email reminders too.

NORFOLK ITEM

30129 082 043 994

NORFOLK COUNTY COUNCIL
LIBRARY AND INFORMATION SERVICE

Also by Neil Campbell

NOVELS
Sky Hooks (Salt 2017)

SHORT STORIES
Broken Doll (Salt 2007)
Pictures from Hopper (Salt 2011)